COMPUTER
GRAPHICS

AUTHORS

R. A. SIDERS

D. R. Drane

L. W. Ehrhardt

P. Ghent

R. G. C. Hanna

C. W. Hayward

W. B. Heye, Jr.

R. A. Meyer

T. G. Rogers, Jr.

J. B. Sabel

COMPUTER

GRAPHICS

Siders

A Revolution in Design

AMERICAN MANAGEMENT ASSOCIATION
NEW YORK

This book has been distributed without charge to AMA members enrolled in the Administrative Services and Research and Development Divisions. Those members who are enrolled in other divisions, or who wish extra copies, may order the book in a hardcover edition at $6 per copy. Price to nonmembers, $9.

Library of Congress catalog card number: 66-24180

This book was originally prepared as a research report submitted in partial fulfillment of the requirements for the Manufacturing Course at the Harvard University Graduate School of Business Administration. The conclusions and opinions expressed herein are those of the authors and do not necessarily represent the views of the Harvard Business School; Professor Georges F. Doriot; or individuals, business corporations, or military or government agencies contacted.

DEDICATION

*To those whose task was to
wait, watch, and work:*

BETSY	MARY
JANET	MELISSA
JEAN	RAE
JOAN	SONJA
JOAN	SUSAN

ACKNOWLEDGMENT

Though the original task was a course project, his vision was never so limited. Though at times we might have faltered, he taught us to reach beyond our grasp. Though we might have done less, he forced us to give more.

As all of his students know, he wants the "epsilon"—the little extra. To the extent that we were able to do this, we gratefully acknowledge the inspiration of Professor Georges F. Doriot.

CONTENTS

Introduction   11

I.   The Power and Potential of Computer Graphics   14

II.   The Engineering Design Cycle   25

III.   The Evolution of Computer Aids to Design   32

IV.   The Role of Passive Computer Graphics   45

V.   The Role of Active Computer Graphics   56

VI.   Who Can Best Use Computer Graphics?   79

VII.   The Economics of the Computer Graphics Decision   84

VIII.   Conditions for Success   109

IX.   The Impact of Computer Graphics on the Company   125

X.   A Plan of Action   137

XI.   A Look at the Future of Computer Graphics   148

Bibliography   157

INTRODUCTION

THE DIGITAL COMPUTER has been on the industrial scene for less than two decades. Despite this brief life, its impact has been widely, if sometimes painfully, felt. Few informed observers today believe this impact has been fully absorbed. Yet the technology of computers and computer applications continues to advance. How can a manager hope to stay abreast of these developments? Even if, for some, the computer has lost its mystery as the result of usage, how can a manager judge the significance and potential value of new and experimental applications?

Without the benefit of a companywide point of view, the computer specialist cannot be expected to make the best decisions on the development of new applications. The best decisions require a peculiar blend of skills. On the one hand, a sound understanding of the technology is needed. On the other hand, the required investment and the organizational and procedural implications call for the best managerial judgment.

Our concern for this problem has led us to examine one computer application that is currently the focus of active technical development—computer graphics as applied to the design process. In the narrowest sense, we are referring to the use of a cathode ray tube, with auxiliary devices connected on-line to a computer. The cathode ray tube is used for graphic communication with the computer for engineering design. Broader definitions of "computer graphics" will become clear later. Those people most actively engaged in this technical development are, quite understandably, very enthusiastic about the potential for such a system. Their enthusiasm and salesmanship require that the manager (1) become familiar with the technology, (2) make a judgment about the implications of that technology for his industry and his company, (3) develop some idea of what benefits can be obtained by capitalizing on the development, (4) define the kind of investment required to obtain the benefits, and (5) decide what actions his company should take in order to realize those benefits that are available at a justifiable cost. It is the purpose of this book to assist in this process.

Although our focus has been narrowed to one specific computer application, it is hoped that the reader will also be able to draw some generalizations which apply to the class of problems of which this is but an example.

To fulfill the purpose of this book, we will examine the evolution of computer aids to engineering design activities and the place of computer graphics in that evolution. The reader will be assisted in judging the applicability of such systems to his company's design activities. Comments will be made on an approach that might be taken to evaluate the investment required and the benefits to be gained. Some critical factors necessary in order to achieve those benefits will be discussed, as well as the implications of such systems for industrial organizations. We feel that little is to be gained by avoiding the stickier issues, and so we will make some projections concerning the technological and sociological developments we expect to see in the future.

Much of the material in this book is pioneering in nature. We are attempting to provide answers to the many questions which a manager would raise concerning the development of a computer graphics capability in the engineering design function of his company. To our knowledge, there has been no other attempt to provide such answers, nor is there available any one source from which such answers can be obtained. We have studied the literature and included a bibliography at the end of this report, which lists what we consider to be the most pertinent references.

The primary source of our data, however, has been interviews with a number of the people most active in, or concerned about, computer graphics in the design process. We sought to determine the point of view of users, university staffs, consultants, computer manufacturers, and military and government representatives. From this body of information, we have pieced together the trends and concepts on which this book is based. In order to properly acknowledge their assistance and to express our gratitude, we list our sources here. The authors, of course, remain solely responsible for the contents of this book.

Professor Steven A. Coons, Timothy Johnson, and Jerome Weiner, Mechanical Engineering Department, Massachusetts Institute of Technology. Thomas Kelly and Robert Cushman, Digigraphic Laboratories, Control Data Corporation. John Allen Jones and Charles Stein, Digital Equipment Corporation. Edward Chase, Charles Adams Associates. Ann

Marie Lamb, Office of Manpower, Automation, and Training, U.S. Department of Labor. M. D. Prince, Research Laboratory, Lockheed-Georgia Company. Dr. Frank Skinner, System Development Laboratory, IBM Corporation. George Edwards, McKinsey and Company. Henry Dreyfuss, Industrial Designer. W. A. McConnell, Charles Missler, Walter Johnson, and William Hogue, Ford Motor Company. Commander Donald Craig, Bureau of Ships, U.S. Navy. Professor Bertram Herzog, Industrial Engineering Department, University of Michigan. Dr. Bernhard Romberg, Arthur D. Little, Inc. James J. Martyniak, O.D. Smith, Jack Gysbers, and D.A. Curtiss, North American Aviation Corporation. Robert Schnuck, Western Region, IBM Corporation. William Fetter and John Freyman, The Boeing Company. Donald E. Hart and Edwin L. Jacks, Research Laboratories, General Motors Corporation. And others who for one reason or another cannot be identified at this time.

The authors wish to express special indebtedness to the faculty and staff of the Harvard University Graduate School of Business Administration. Professor F. Warren McFarlan contributed substantially to the economic concepts considered. Finally, we wish to express our gratitude to Thomas Burke and his associates at the Computer Research Laboratory, National Aeronautics and Space Administration, Cambridge, Massachusetts, for substantially alleviating the financial burdens associated with our research.

CHAPTER I

THE POWER AND POTENTIAL OF COMPUTER GRAPHICS •

It was a warm june afternoon as Denton Smart drove to see his old friend Ralph Morris, vice president of the Helverson Manufacturing Company. Morris had suggested that Denton come to see the way in which the Helverson Engineering Department was using computer graphics to design the many new products it developed each year. This was of particular interest to Denton because the company for which he worked was very interested in installing such a system and felt that it would be to the company's advantage to have someone visit a working installation before it committed itself to this radical new application.

He met Ralph at 2:00 p.m., and Ralph took him straight to the R&D labs to see Charles Ferris, who was the company's most experienced computer-aided designer.

"Charles, I would like you to meet Denton Smart from United. He is interested in our computer-aided design setup and would like as much information about it as you can give him. If you two don't mind, I'll leave you to it. Drop in to my office and see me before you go, Denton, and I'll try to answer any questions you may have after Charles has shown you how we use the system."

Charles took Denton out into the Engineering Lab and showed him the equipment they used in their design process. He had to admit he was a little disappointed. All he saw were several pieces of equipment that looked like desks with television sets mounted on them. On the left of each desk was a box containing about 30 push buttons, while in the middle of the desk was what looked like a fountain pen, connected to the main equipment by a flexible electric cable.

"These are the terminals through which we talk to the computer," began Charles.

"Whereabouts is the computer?" Denton interrupted. "Is it in the next room?"

"No," Charles laughed, "it's actually in the headquarters building about a mile from here. These terminals are connected to it by cable, but, for all intents and purposes, it could be in the next room, because every time we use this equipment we have instant access to the main processor. In fact, we operate on a real-time basis from here. This means that one central machine does all the data processing for the company, payroll, production scheduling, our design work—in fact, the lot. Now that Joe over there has finished using that terminal, why don't we take over and I'll actually do a design of the motor mounting bracket for our new model X52 that we plan to release next year. This is the last piece of that design; so we will also be able to simulate our first 'prototype' test on the console. I'll explain what I'm doing as I go along, but stop me if there is anything you don't understand."

Denton pulled up a spare chair and sat down beside Charles, who readied himself at the console.

"The first thing I'll do," he said, "is to call up the drawings of the parts with which this bracket has to mate." So saying, he pushed a button which caused a master listing of code numbers and drawing descriptions to be displayed on the screen.

"Where did this information come from?" Denton asked.

"It's kept on random-access magnetic files at our central computer along with digital replicas of all our thousands and thousands of engineering drawings. I can see from this listing that the part drawings associated with the motor bracket are these three here." He indicated three of the numbers that were displayed on the screen and continued, "Now, if I want to see one of these drawings, I simply point the light pen at the code number and press this recall button." A complete engineering drawing appeared on the screen.

"What's this light pen that you're talking about?" Denton interrupted the engineer.

"Oh, that's this pen-like thing here," he said, as he waved his right hand. "It's connected to the console by a cable and is sensitive to the light glowing on the screen. When I hold it close to the screen like this [he pointed the pen at the screen from a distance of about a quarter of an inch], the computer knows that I am interested in that particular part of the display. In this case it is the code number for a drawing, and the computer program knows that when I push the recall button it should display that specific drawing on the screen."

"So that's what a light pen is," Denton said. "I've often heard about them but never seen one work. It's really extremely clever."

"Not only clever but very useful to the designer," replied Charles. "It means that we can talk to the computer by drawing on the screen. Graphics, it's called, but more of that later. I'll now call all three of those motor bracket drawings onto the screen at once and have them arranged in separate corners of the display." He proceeded to point the pen and push the recall button.

"There we are. Now I will position these three parts in an exact scale relationship to each other. This relationship is determined by an overall layout drawing that the computer has filed away." He pushed a button that was marked "Constraint," and instantaneously the three separate part outlines shuffled themselves on the screen and took up the dimensional position that they would assume in the final product.

"Now," said Charles, "all I have to do is design the bracket that will hold these three parts together. There are many other parts in the complete unit, but I only need to know about these three in order to design the motor bracket." He proceeded to sketch in his conception of a suitable bracket by using the light pen and the push buttons.

"How do you draw those lines?" Denton asked.

"It's really quite simple," Charles replied. "I direct the light pen to the point at which I wish to start the line, push the 'line' button on this box and then move the pen to the point where the line should end. The computer generated a line that is like a glowing thread attached to the tip of the pen. See, I can move it all over the screen. Now, if I want it to end here I quickly move the pen away, and there we have a line. I can do the same sort of thing to draw circles, squares, and all sorts of shapes. I don't have to be too careful, because the computer will automatically straighten lines, circularize circles, and so on. This saves a terrific amount of time in this drafting type of work. No more T-squares, compasses, or sharp pencils are required. In fact, we have reduced our total design time by a factor of 12. Some projects that used to take three years can now be done in three months!"

Charles continued sketching in the bracket, mating bolt holes here, showing welded joints there. Denton was particularly impressed by the way he put into the bracket a series of equal-sized holes and remarked, "I notice that you only drew one of those circular holes and then, by some magic, repeated the hole in several places. Is that something special?"

"Not for computer graphics," replied Charles. "Having drawn it once, I can repeat it as often as I like. Very handy for drawing gear wheels! All I need to do is draw one tooth, and then I can repeat it as often as is necessary to complete the gear. Well, I think this bracket is finished now. You'll have noticed that in this case I used my experience to decide how thick the sections would need to be in order for the bracket not to fail when the product is in use. In the old days I would have allowed plenty of strength here and probably have overengineered the part to alleviate the possibility of failure under stress. Now I can use the computer to simulate the tryout of this model under actual operating conditions, which of course allows us to detect shortcomings in the design before we build a prototype. It used to get very expensive building several prototypes one after the other before we made all the necessary modifications and ironed out all the bugs. However, before we do proceed with the tryout, I'd better call up from the computer the total design and see if this bracket interferes with any of the electrical wiring or metal parts that the boys in the other labs in the building may have designed into the product."

Charles then proceeded to display a complete picture of the finished product. He gave an anguished grunt and said, "Look, I've clamped that bracket right over one of the main cables in the system. I forgot that was there, but I think I can get over it by cutting a notch in the bracket. It is really fantastic how we can now have designers working on the same product all over the company and yet avoid putting a fuel line right through a hydraulic pipe. We used to find out this type of thing only when we had almost completed the first prototype. Well, anyway, I'd better alter this bracket to allow for the cable."

Charles made all the necessary alterations and leaned back with a satisfied sigh. "All done now," he said. "The last piece designed and the whole product completed. Let's try it out and see if it works."

"I am afraid you'll have to explain to me how you are going to simulate the operation of this product on a computer," Denton exclaimed.

"Well, the capability for doing this sort of thing was one of our most difficult hurdles," replied Charles. "We got over it by letting the computer do most of the work for us. In setting up a simulation of this type there are a great number of factors to be considered; so many, in fact, that it would have taken years for our programmers to tell the computer how to go about performing the test. Nowadays we use these consoles to actually program the computer. We draw the program flow charts on the screen and then call up 'packets' of generalized programs which we piece together to build up a total program. Because each 'packet' contains a whole series of steps that are already programmed and in the computer files, we don't have to recalculate every step each time we want to make a new type of test."

"It sounds to me like using a set of building blocks and piecing them together in a variety of different ways in order to have the computer do the different tasks you want," Denton replied.

"Exactly," said Charles. "We have a library of building blocks from which we select the ones we need to build the particular program we are after. It allows us to be flexible and to do the job quickly at the same time. However, we have already built the program for this type of product; so it is simply a matter of testing it now." So saying, he manipulated the buttons until everything was displayed on the screen ready for tryout.

"Here we go," said Charles, and shafts and wheels started to turn. "Better speed it up to 150 percent of normal to try and accelerate the test." Charles pointed the light pen at an rpm chart displayed on the right of the screen. "Five thousand revs should do it. Now, by watching this stress chart on the left and pointing by pen at the point I want the stress calculated for, I can see if a part is being overloaded. I'll just check my bracket and see how it's standing up. Well, the stress figures look O.K. It should be good, but I'll hand it over to Joe and let him carry out a full analysis. So there you are—computer-aided design at work."

"It's really astonishing," Denton responded, "but now what happens to the drawings that are in the computer files? How do you use them?"

"Well, if the simulated tests appear to be all right, then we will make up a prototype by using the digitized drawing information that is in the files to run numerically controlled machine tools. These will produce all the necessary parts and allow us to construct a solid model. Actually, we don't often put the drawing information out on paper any more, although we can get the computer to plot it out for us. By keeping the information in the computer, we are always up to date with the latest modifications, and consequently we can avoid having people working from obsolete drawings. They just call on the computer and have a look at the latest version. In the old days, the continuous modifying and redistributing of drawings was extremely expensive."

"Do you use these graphic consoles for anything else besides mechanical work?" Denton asked.

"Oh, yes!" Charles replied. "We do electronic circuit design and analysis, simulate hydraulic systems—in fact almost all phases of engineering. The other day I heard that our plant engineering fellows had installed a console to allow them to do the architecture for our new factory. There seems to be no end to it, although I must admit we haven't reached the stage where the computer will think up the new ideas regarding what products we should build. I doubt if it ever will, thank goodness. They will always need us designers to do the really creative work, although draftsmen, as such, are a disappearing race."

"Well, Charles," said Denton, "I have found this extremely interesting and you have done a very good job of selling me on the idea of developing our own system. Before I get completely carried away, however, I really need to get down to brass tacks and find out how I would actually go about deciding the size of system we need, whether it would pay off for us, and what effect it would have on *our* design staff and *our* organization as a whole.

THE QUESTIONS RAISED

This imaginary story illustrates the *power* and *potential* of computer graphics as applied to the design process. We must admit that a system with all the capabilities described above does not currently exist, although it is our firm belief that the facilities described will in fact become a reality in the foreseeable future.

However, the story also serves the purpose of this report proper, which is to raise, answer, and elaborate on the type of questions that management will be asking and, in so doing, to present to the manager a nontechnical evaluation of the factors relevant to the development of a computer graphics facility.

The obvious first question is just what is computer graphics? The term computer graphics refers to the concept of man communicating with a computer *by means of graphical symbols such as lines, curves, dots, and so forth.* Of course, alphabetical or numerical symbols can also be involved, but the concept goes far beyond them. In a sense, computer graphics can be considered as one more degree of freedom in man-machine communication. Communication with a computer has traditionally been limited to punched cards or tape and typewriter input, with some kind of printing device being the normal output. Optical scanners and magnetic character coders have been restricted to the recognition of limited sets of characters. Computer graphics now adds the dimension of sketching and drawing for both input to *and* output from the computer. One need only reflect on the old saw, "A picture is worth a thousand words," to grasp the significance of this new dimension.

The actual devices associated with computer graphics include a variety of cathode ray tubes, plotters, recorders, and scanners. Our focus here will be predominantly on the cathode ray tube as a graphical communication device, because of the significance of being able to *draw directly on the scope face* and of thus communicating with the computer in a form not restricted to a set of alphabetical, numerical, or special characters—and without the necessity of an intermediate medium. Similarly, the computer is able to *display* graphical information for interpretation by the man. The flexibility and high rate of information transfer (as opposed to mere data transfer) presented by such freedom of communication is not likely to be surpassed until it is possible to interact meaningfully with a computer by physically talking to it and receiving a spoken reply. Such a capability is being studied, but is not likely to be of significance in the foreseeable future.

Computer graphics has a large number of other uses besides its use in engineering design, and in a later chapter we will consider a number of them. We will concentrate, however, on relating the concept of computer graphics to its use in the engineering design process. Unless otherwise indicated, then, the reader should assume that when we use the term computer graphics, we mean the use of graphical communication with a computer to assist the *design* function.

Many other terms have been coined and are being used to describe this and similar processes: Automated Design Engineering (ADE), Machine Aided Cognition (MAC), Computer Augmentation of the Human Intellect, Design Augmented by Computer (DAC), Computer-Aided Design (CAD), and Digigraphics are among the more popular. All of these terms tend to be broader than the definition we seek—some by including all applications of computer graphics, not just design, and some by including all forms of computer assistance to design, not just graphical. It is that area which is common to both classes which is our concern. Our difficulties with terminology do not end there, however, because our research indicates that a subdivision of computer graphics into its "active" and "passive" forms is a useful distinction to make. These terms, however, will be made clear later.

Much material has been written concerning the burgeoning field of computer graphics, from the early descriptions of the M.I.T. SKETCH-PAD system[1] to the ever increasing number of reports issued by many of the larger companies, such as Lockheed Aircraft Corporation and

---

[1] Sutherland, I. E., "SKETCHPAD—A Man-Machine Graphical Communication System," *Proceedings—Spring Joint Computer Conference, 1963,* Spartan Books, Inc., Baltimore, 1963.

General Motors. The thrust of this material has been technical in nature and, as such, has been aimed at the systems engineer and computer specialist. In this book, however, we intend to explore this subject from the point of view of the manager in a technically oriented company—one who would be responsible for proposing or approving projects for the use of computer graphics as an aid to the design process or who simply wants to learn more about it.

THE POWER OF COMPUTER GRAPHICS

The power of computer graphics when applied to the design cycle is far-reaching. It results from the imaginative application of the unique capabilities of the computer and graphical equipment to design problems. This power has been likened to the "synergy" (united action) or "2 + 2 = 5" effect, the concept being that by allowing the designer to do what he can do best, and by having the computer perform the tasks for which it is best suited, then the resulting effect is greater than the sum of the two parts. There are many people who are convinced that such a result is in fact possible. M. D. Prince, associate director of research, System Sciences, at Lockheed-Georgia, where a significant effort in computer graphics has been under way for several years, speaks of this unusual effect as follows:

> Man-computer synergism is made possible by the freely flowing interchange of information between the man and the computer. That is, the barrier between man and computer has been broken down so that a "real time conversation" can take place. This man-computer conversation has been made possible by recent advances in the speed of the digital computer, methods and techniques of programming, and the development of auxiliary input-output apparatus. The "conversation" may be in the form of typed messages, figures and symbols drawn on a television-like display, or other suitable forms which are acceptable both to the man and the machine.[2]

The logical basis for this concept lies in the fact that the human mind tends to problem-solve heuristically while a computer problem-solves by the use of algorithms—that is, the human mind arrives at practical solutions by trial and error, while the computer arrives at precise solutions by following an error-free sequence of logic. Both types of solution are needed in many design problems; and thus by allowing both man and machine to work efficiently on that part of the problem for which they

[2] Prince, M. D., S. H. Chasen, *et al.*, "Computer-Aided Design," *Lockheed-Georgia Quarterly*, Summer 1965.

are best suited, a result better than the sum of the individual efforts is obtained—a result that is considerably enhanced by the use of instantaneous graphical displays in man-machine communication. Thus the synergy effect demonstrates the potential power of computer graphics in the design process.

THE POTENTIAL OF COMPUTER GRAPHICS

The potential for imaginative use of computer graphics is evident in many ways. Some applications are readily available today, while others —although conceptually possible—will require more development before they become feasible as working tools for the designer. We plan to illustrate this potential at this point by mentioning only some of the many ways in which computer graphics will markedly affect the design function of the company, while leaving a more detailed study to a later chapter.

One major benefit of computer graphics is the possibility of substantial reduction in the time required for the design process. Many claims have been made for this, and our company interviews and research indicate that drastic reductions in time requirements are realistically possible. It is felt in the automotive industry, for example, that a full-fledged computer graphics system might decrease the design time for a new automobile from two years to around three or four months. Dr. Bernhard Romberg of Arthur D. Little estimates that the new, only partially automated, design system for the U.S. Navy will cut ship detail design time from eighteen months to anywhere from two to four weeks. Lockheed-Georgia has ready for production use a three-console computer graphics system for two-dimensional numerical control parts programming, and unofficial estimates place the reduction in parts programming time from this program to be on the order of 6 to 1. It is thus clear that currently available computer graphics systems allow for considerable reduction in time requirements, and it can be safely predicted that the more advanced systems of future years will make possible the production of designs in even less time.

Another benefit from the use of computer graphics systems occurs in those problems known as "interference" problems. These difficulties arise in the course of the more complicated projects where it is necessary to have many designers working on the same project at once. At present, the discovery that a planned hydraulic pipe will pass right through the middle of a gas line is generally made during the construction of the first prototype. The problems of systems interference materialize in many other wonderful and varied guises, but the concept of computer graphics has the potential to enable designers to eliminate or substantially reduce the incidence of such setbacks.

A major benefit will be the reduction in errors arising from the use of outdated drawings. As any design department will testify, the continuous modification and updating of countless drawings is a tedious chore at best, and despite the elaborate control systems devised to prevent the use of old drawings, there are many instances of the arrival in the plant of parts which have been made to "Issue 2" rather than to "Issue 3" of a drawing. One large aerospace company estimates that 20 percent of the activity in relation to any drawing is the initial preparation and 80 percent is correction and change. Another large aerospace company more conservatively places the ratio at 50:50. In any event, computer graphics, by maintaining a readily accessible and continuously updated master file of drawings, could eliminate or at least seriously reduce this source of error and wasted time once and for all.

The time savings and increase in efficiency occasioned by the unique nature of computer graphics is another benefit. This is the ability to try out many more solutions to any given design problem than was previously possible. Thus the potential exists for better designs and more of them. In fact, the ability for increased customizing is available to the company which seeks to use individuality of content or styling as a powerful product marketing tool. In discussing this advantage, IBM said that some people view computer graphics primarily as a means to shorten the design cycle, while others view computer graphics as a means of achieving more during the present design cycle. The former usage of the time made available by computer graphics is in our opinion of benefit to those industries where competitive advantage lies in rapid response to consumer tastes. The latter usage of the time made available by computer graphics is important, on the other hand, to the aerospace companies, where high-performance designs are required. Whatever the advantage to any particular company, it is clear that computer graphics will allow more design activities to be accomplished in a given period of time.

It is also possible to visualize the time when, through computer graphics, there will be a minimum of hard-copy drawings, as they are known today. All call-up of drawings—even by the subcontractor across town—will be carried out on a visual display terminal linked to the central computer. There is also the likelihood that at least some of the output of the computer will be in the form of numerically controlled machine-tool tapes that can be placed directly on the production machines. Once again a possible source of error—that of reading and interpreting drawings—will have been eliminated.

These benefits would appear to be only a prelude to what we can expect to see emerging in the future. It is our opinion that the potential of computer graphics is only just beginning to be tapped. There is no denying the complexity and difficulty of implementing a computer graphics system given the present state of the art. The potential payoffs, as we plan to show in the chapters ahead, suggest that it is nevertheless well worthwhile for management to give serious attention *now* to the implications of this concept for their own organizations.

As the result of our research, three major conclusions have emerged and are worthy of mention at this point in the report, since they provide the rationale for pursuing the topic in greater depth:

1. Computer graphics is *today* important for large companies with annual sales greater than, say, $1 billion.

2. The full potential of computer graphics has not yet been realized but in any event should be available for solving even *unstructured* design problems in most small companies—$5-10 million in sales —by 1975.

3. Computer graphics, though difficult to implement in any company, promises big payoffs, both economic and intangible.

CHAPTER II

THE ENGINEERING DESIGN CYCLE •

IN ORDER TO UNDERSTAND the role that computer graphics is presently playing in the design cycle, we must first understand the *process* of engineering design and the role the computer has played in design. Even more importantly, a thorough understanding of these matters will permit us to better judge the impact computer graphics can—and someday will—have on this function.

The design process as we are dealing with it here is, of course, an abstraction. There are as many design processes as there are design groups, and no two are identical. In order to discuss the subject meaningfully, then, we need something of a general case. If our description includes the significant characteristics more frequently encountered, we will avoid emphasizing, while not eliminating, the special case.

A particularly useful description of the design process has been articulated by Professors Robert W. Mann and Steven A. Coons of the Mechanical Engineering Department at M.I.T. This chapter draws heavily on their description as presented by Professor Mann to the University of Michigan-University of Detroit Engineering Summer Conference in August 1964. A graphical representation of the design process as described by Mann and Coons appears in Exhibit 1. This chapter also draws on the thinking of people we interviewed.

The design process starts when a need has been perceived and the organization has adopted the fulfillment of that need as a goal. The need may be for a space vehicle, a bridge to span the Chesapeake, a new model of last year's Pontiac, or a camera capable of instant photography.

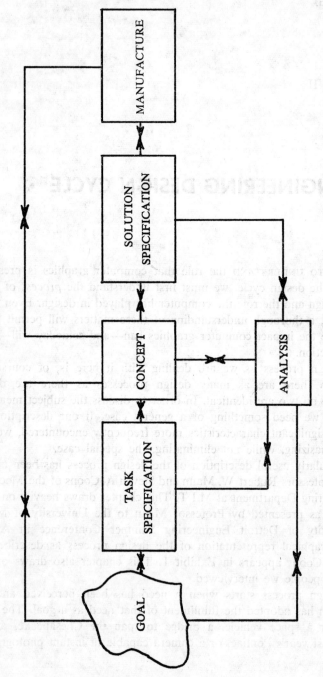

THE ENGINEERING DESIGN PROCESS

Source: Presentation by Robert W. Mann, Professor of Mechanical Engineering, M.I.T., to the University of Michigan-University of Detroit Engineering Summer Conference, August 3-7, 1964.

EXHIBIT 1

The designer's first job is to delineate the task in as specific and quantitative a fashion as is possible. Such task specifications normally describe the performance required or desired and serve as guidelines for activity to follow and as criteria for judging the degree of success that has been achieved when the final design is complete.

To proceed further requires an idea for a possible solution of the problem. This is the creative phase of design. The engineer draws on his experience and knowledge to formulate a concept which may satisfy the specifications. The concept, initially quite vague and ephemeral, firms up as information is gathered and the tentative solution is filled in with detail. It's possible that the original goal may be modified: either expanded because the designer has exceeded the requirements and the increased performance has been found to be desirable or reduced because the best concepts for a solution just can't meet the original requirements.

In any case, the process being described does not generally occur in a simple, sequential fashion. At each subsequent step it is possible that prior decisions may have to be changed and a new sequence started. In the case of designing a space vehicle such an iterative process is likely to occur to a greater extent than when designing a new model automobile because of the tentative and uncertain nature of space-vehicle design problems. Especially in the former case, the flash of creativity is likely to occur at random and unpredictable intervals. Indeed, it is quite possible in design groups for a concept to emerge seemingly quite accidentally and then for a search for an appropriate goal to follow.

The concept must then be evaluated by a process of analysis. It is subjected to both qualitative, intuitive judgment and to very precise quantitative analysis. The esthetic value of the proposed design is evaluated in a purely judgmental fashion, whereas its ability to withstand stress might be evaluated by a mathematical process. This sharpening of the concept, once again, can lead to a re-specifying of the concept or of the task or even of the initial goal.

The process of conceptualization and analysis are carried out through the medium of a graphical representation. As a result, when they have been completed, we most often find that the specification of the solution is largely complete. The drawings, specifications, manufacturing information, and so forth have been developed. Manufacturing considerations have overlapped the conceptual and analytical stages. Production engineering has imposed its analysis on the product and required, if necessary, modifications of the concept, the task specification, and perhaps even the original goal.

The entire process, we have seen, is characterized by iteration. Subsequent analysis, or information unearthed at some point downstream, can suggest or require that a previous, tentative decision be modified. This is especially characteristic of the interplay between conceptualization and analysis. The conceptualization of a solution is a flash of creativity. It doesn't last long in relation to the overall time scale. The analysis, on the other hand, tends to be a lengthy, mechanical process and does not leave much opportunity for creativity. As results are available from the analysis, however, they may spark a fresh creative moment. A new, tentative concept is formulated and must be subjected to further lengthy analysis. This concept is analogous to a signal on an oscilloscope, where the random peaks might correspond to creative moments. Such iteration is, realistically, only limited by the pressures of time or budget.

Design problems tend to be hierarchical; that is, there are really several levels of problems. If the entire product can be called a system, then it is composed of components, each made up of elements. Our straightforward description of the design process has not yet recognized that the process proceeds at many levels at once. At the "systems" level, a ship might have a specified overall length, gross weight, speed in knots, and so on. At the "component" level, a power plant might be required to deliver a specified horsepower while consuming a given fuel below a given rate. At the "element" level, an individual boiler might have to generate a specified steam pressure within certain constraints of space and vessel strength. Once the grosser level has been specified, the lesser can be specified. At each level there is opportunity for creativity, and there is a set of appropriate analyses to be conducted. At each level, iteration occurs between concept and analysis. A change of concept at one level can readily require modifications at the same or other levels.

Another way of viewing the design process is as a series of decisions. From the very beginning, alternatives are being evaluated and commitments made. The larger decisions regarding the goal, task specification, and overall design concepts are made first and, as the process continues, the decisions tend to be at the lower levels in the hierarchy concerned with lesser concepts. The commitment to a specific course of action becomes stronger and stronger as the decisions accumulate. Flexibility is lost, not because it is impossible to change an early, major decision but because time and budget limitations won't always permit it.

The number of people involved in the design project increases. From the initial activities of a few highly skilled designers, the project grows to include groups addressing the problems associated with the design of the systems, the components, and, eventually, the elements. The level of skills required decreases as the less creative activities associated with element design and solution specification are undertaken. Since a multitude of efforts are proceeding in parallel, problems of communication and coordination occur. A modification in the weapons system of a ship alters the requirements for the electrical system, for example. Such changes will have implications for the degree to which the original goal will be fulfilled. Perhaps the change will result in too high a cost of manufacture. There is an increasing *need,* therefore, for control and coordination at the same time as the *problems* of control and coordination are increasing.

As the number of people engaged in the activity increases, as time passes, and as materials and supplies are consumed, the funds committed to date to the project increase. The *rate* of cash exposure increases. The result is an increasing costly consequence should the result be less than satisfactory. Of course, the uncertainty regarding the satisfactory nature of the result declines as the design is firmed up and more analyses of the expected performance are conducted.

The rest of the organization, outside of design, becomes increasingly engaged as the design process continues and nears completion. Marketing establishes forecasts for sales and prepares the merchandising themes and distribution plans. Manufacturing establishes schedules for production. Capital expenditures are made to prepare the plant facilities and equipment required for the forecasted volume. Purchasing seeks sources of supply. Subcontracting bids are sought. Personnel forecasts the number and skills required by the production force. Hiring and training are carried out. The organization prepares for the day when the design process culminates in a torrent of output specifying the solution of the design problem. All these nondesign activities add significantly to the financial consequences of being wrong and to the inflexibility for change.

Of course, the design process doesn't really end there. Despite the extensive analyses and the building and testing of prototypes, the final product test occurs in the hands of customers or users. Modifications and refinements may be required. The need may have shifted, requiring a partial redesign. Some of these concepts are presented graphically in Exhibit 2.

So far, we've been viewing the design process as though we were external to it. It may be worthwhile at this point to place ourselves within it and consider the process from the viewpoint of a single participant, the engineer.

The engineer is given a piece of the problem to solve: perhaps it is

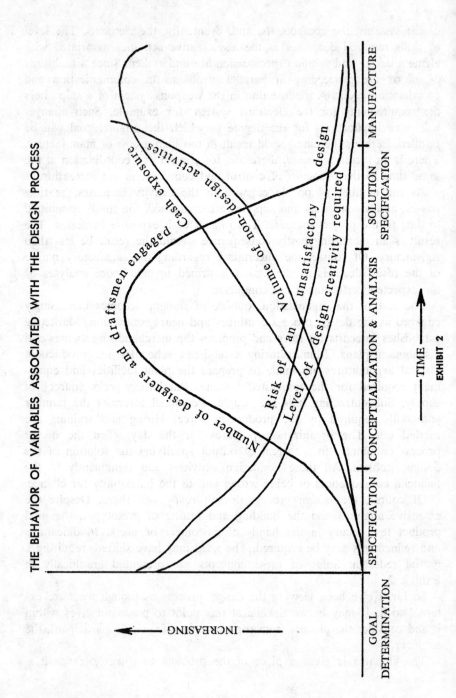

THE BEHAVIOR OF VARIABLES ASSOCIATED WITH THE DESIGN PROCESS

EXHIBIT 2

just one element in the hierarchy. The design specifications define the desired performance. After immersing himself in the relevant information, the engineer thinks about the problem until he is able to conceptualize a solution. He proceeds to carry out a number of lengthy, fairly mechanical analyses. As the results of the analyses become available, he may be prompted to a fresh surge of creativity. A new round of lengthy analysis ensues. On occasion, he will encounter an element of the design that cannot be handled by drawing on the physical principles at his disposal. In that case he draws on experience, intuition, and judgment to arrive at a satisfactory solution.

As he proceeds, he draws on standards made available for his use and guidance. Standard parts are used. Physical properties of materials, characteristics of electronic components, manufacturing standards—all are made available. Also, as he proceeds, he will be recording his design. Initially very rough and undetailed, his drawings will gradually become more and more complete.

Occasionally he will be notified that adjacent elements have been changed or that the constraints within which he has been working have been altered. He may have to adapt to new specifications of his product's task. Eventually, time pressures will dictate that his solution be firmed up and final documentation prepared.

Now we can turn to the salient features of the design process:

- It is an iterative process.
- Brief, unpredictable moments of creativity are interspersed with lengthy analyses.
- Intuition and judgment are brought to bear when quantitative, physical techniques fail or are inappropriate.
- Choices between alternatives are constantly being made—first major, then more minor.
- The process proceeds iteratively at a number of levels in the hierarchy.
- The number of people and disciplines increases; problems of communication, coordination, and integration mount.
- Other functional areas of the business become increasingly engaged as the process progresses.
- The cash exposure to the project increases, the cost of change mounts, and flexibility is lost.
- Standards are introduced as aids and controls.
- The design is recorded in increasing detail, primarily in graphical form, for subsequent manufacture.

CHAPTER III

THE EVOLUTION OF COMPUTER
AIDS TO DESIGN •

Having established a framework for discussing the engineering design process, we are ready to consider the evolution of computer aids to that process. In this chapter we will recount the course that computer assistance has followed, the obstacles that have been encountered, and some of the means that have been devised for overcoming them. We will describe some of the computer programs that have been developed and relate them to our concept of the design process.

THE BASIS FOR COMPUTER USE IN DESIGN

The encroachment of the computer into the design process has progressed steadily since its inception. The particular attributes the computer possesses include speed, memory, and reliability. A computer performs computations and makes logical decisions at a rate that is difficult to comprehend. Its memory is capable of storing data and making use of those data as instructed. It performs these functions in an extremely reliable fashion, as indeed it must since the tremendous volume of operations performed in a given length of time make unacceptable anything less.

Since the most obvious capability of the computer is to compute, it was to the task of computation that the machine was first put. The processing of payroll and accounting data is still a typical first application in most companies. In the design function, computation occurs during the process of analysis. It is by no means the whole of analysis, since this function also includes the structuring of a model of the concept, the determination of the pertinent physical principles, and the conducting of experiments to determine performance. The solving of equations and the manipulation of data, nevertheless, play a large part in the analytical procedure.

From the beginning, however, the engineer has been confronted by two obstacles. The first is the problem of communicating with the computer. The second is the availability of the computer with respect to time and physical location.

LANGUAGE AND COMMUNICATION

Prior to 1957, the engineer had to learn machine language in order to express his computations in a form that could be input to the computer. Besides the burdensome chore represented by the learning process, such a restriction on the means of communication meant that the engineer had to recast his problems in a form that was expressible in the machine's limited vocabulary. Every step of the process had to be reduced to the level of addition, subtraction, and equality comparisons. Useful pre-coded packets were, of course, developed; but their generality and, therefore, usefulness was limited.

The time-consuming chore of recasting the desired procedure into a suitable form could be given to a computer programmer; but if the engineer did not know programming and the programmer was not familiar with engineering, the process was susceptible to gross error and frustration.

A significant advance occurred in 1957 with the introduction of FORTRAN (FORmula TRANslator) developed by J. W. Bachus and associates at IBM. This higher-level language allowed the engineer to express his problems in algebraic terms, which he more readily understood. FORTRAN is representative of a number of higher-level languages that were developed. Its eventual predominant usage resulted as much from its IBM sponsorship as it did from its virtues. FORTRAN was not a problem-oriented language; that is, it was not structured to facilitate the expression of problems in any specific engineering discipline. Further, the task of defining and managing the data on which to operate was left in the hands of the engineer, and the vagaries of data management remained his problem. Despite these drawbacks, FORTRAN represented a major step toward making the computer a useful tool for the engineer. Computer usage soared as engineers, becoming more familiar with computers and having a language they could more easily use, conceived new and more ambitious applications. More and more computational chores were relegated to the machine, and computations not previously possible were undertaken. The determination of the applications to be undertaken was now made by engineers as well as computer specialists.

We have stated that FORTRAN was not a problem-oriented language, at least as we have defined the term. In an effort to bring the computer more readily to bear on specific problems in particular disciplines, such problem-oriented languages have been developed. An example is COGO (COordinate GeOmetry), designed for the solution of civil engineering problems and developed by Professor C. L. Miller of M.I.T. in 1960. The impact of COGO on the civil engineering profession has been substantial. This language facilitates the expression of civil engineering problems in fewer words and in less time than was possible with FORTRAN. Exhibit 1 contrasts a COGO routine to FORTRAN and machine-language routines performing the same function. The fact that the language includes a vocabulary natural to the civil engineer eliminates the previously existing requirement that he recast his solution in computer-oriented terms. The impact of COGO is reflected in a statement by Daniel Roos: "One state highway department uses COGO for over 50% of their computer runs. The one COGO system supersedes several hundred special purpose geometric programs."[1]

Other problem-oriented languages have been developed. STRESS (STRuctural Engineering System Solver) was developed by the Department of Civil Engineering at M.I.T. Similarly, SEPOL was developed for soil engineering.

These and other problem-oriented languages have helped to overcome the obstacle to communication with the computer that the engineer previously faced, even with FORTRAN. They too suffer from shortcomings, however, because, while they more nearly match the natural problem-expressing form of the engineer, they still fall short of a truly natural form. The engineer works in graphical terms as well as in mathematical terms. When he has to translate his graphical expression (perhaps a drawing) into a linear stream of letters, numbers, and special characters, he (1) is using up time, (2) is likely to make errors not always easily detected, and (3) is not being creative, at least not in a design sense.

[1] Roos, Daniel, *ICES System Design*, Technical Report T65-8, Department of Civil Engineering, Massachusetts Institute of Technology, August 20, 1965, p. 5.

PERFORMING A SIMPLE FUNCTION WITH A COMPUTER

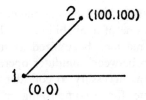

This is the way an engineer would solve a simple problem using a computer. Three programming languages are shown—COGO/QUIKTRAN, FORTRAN, and machine language.

To be determined is the distance between points 1 and 2.

COGO/QUIKTRAN:

```
           STORE 1       0.000   0.000
           STORE 2       100.000   100.000
           DISTANCE      1 2
Response:                1 2   141.4214
```

FORTRAN:

```
           XCORD1 = 0.000
           YCORD1 = 0.000
           XCORD2 = 100.000
           YCORD2 = 100.000
           DIST12 = SQRTF( (XCORD2−XCORD1)**2
                          +(YCORD2−YCORD1)**2)
     No immediate response
```

Machine Language:

```
        XCORD1     FLBIN              0
        YCORD1     FLBIN              0
        XCORD2     FLBIN            100
        YCORD2     FLBIN            100
        TEMP1      FLBIN              0
        TEMP2      FLBIN              0
                   FBS       XCORD2     XCORD1     TEMP1
                   FBS       YCORD2     YCORD1     TEMP2
                   FBM       TEMP1      TEMP1      TEMP1
                   FBM       TEMP2      TEMP2      TEMP2
                   FBA       TEMP1      TEMP2      TEMP1
                   L,SQRT               TEMP1
     No immediate response
```

EXHIBIT 1

AVAILABILITY IN TIME AND SPACE

The second major obstacle faced by the engineer, in his quest to make use of the computer, was one of availability. The high costs of equipment rentals dictated that the machine be utilized as fully as possible. Rather than view the relationship between computer operation and user from the user's point of view, it was necessary to consider the machine first. As a result, the typical scheme for accomplishing maximum utilization has been to adopt batch processing methods. The problems of a number of users are batched together and run as a single unit.

The frustrations of batch processing for the engineer are many. He conceives of a problem for which he needs computer assistance, or he hears of a program someone else has written which he'd like to use. He establishes the computational methodology that should be followed to achieve his solution. Every eventuality must be anticipated and provided for. He structures the methodology in a form that is acceptable as input to the computer, perhaps using a problem-oriented language. He submits his run, which usually means he puts it in a box at a collection point. He doesn't expect the run back for two, four, or six hours; so he turns his attention to another problem. His run comes back (a pile of printer output and his card deck are delivered), and he finds that his input had a misplaced card. He corrects the problem and resubmits the run. Several hours later, or the next day, it is returned and he discovers that the program ran but that he had specified some parameters so that the solutions are outside the area of interest. He reaches this conclusion only after re-thinking the problem—he's been away from it for a full day. Determined to get a useful answer on the next run, he increases the number of parameters to be used for calculation and resubmits the job. Several hours later his run is returned. On top is a nasty note from the computation center supervisor suggesting that 30 minutes of computer time and a three-inch pile of printer output appear excessive. He digs into the pile, finds the four or five pages with pertinent information and discards the rest. Now he has to plow through the numbers—quite possibly graphing the data to make them meaningful—and he has the answer he sought. Pondering the answer, he conceives of an alternative design that might better fit the specifications. To check it out, he once again starts the process of preparing a program for computer solution.

The problem of computer availability has been recognized for a long time. It has not been a problem peculiar to engineering design. A great deal of progress has been made in developing schemes to solve the problem. These schemes have centered around the use of remote terminals for input and output to the computer and the development of computer monitoring procedures which permit the machine to respond to remote inquiries on a "real-time" basis.

We should note at this point some of the recent advances in this area. Project MAC at M.I.T. is widely known for its progress in the development of time-shared systems. A time-shared system is one in which the computer services a number of remote terminals, scanning the active stations according to some scheduling algorithm, and alloting sufficient equipment and processing time to each in turn, so that to each user it appears that he has full, continuous use of the computer's capabilities. A similar system has been developed at Dartmouth on General Electric equipment, and terminals are in user's hands around the country.

Another method for servicing remote terminals in real time is by use of a "multiprogramming" scheme. This approach assumes that a significant portion of the computer's time will be spent on batch processing operations. Provision is made for the batch mode to be interrupted by a call from a remote terminal. The call is serviced, usually to some logical stopping point, and the batch mode resumes. Effective implementation of this concept has been widely achieved. Since not all computer jobs require real-time operation (for example, payroll), this approach is an effective alternative.

IBM has combined the COGO system with QUIKTRAN, a time-sharing system. It is described as ". . . a remote, time-sharing conversational programming language for civil engineers."[2] The system uses an IBM 1050 data communication terminal which is connected by telephone line to a nearby computer facility. By means of QUIKTRAN the engineer can communicate from a remote typewriter in a conversational mode in COGO language. By combining time-sharing operation with a problem-oriented language the computer has been brought a step closer to a natural relationship with the designer.

Daniel Roos of the M.I.T. Civil Engineering Systems Laboratory, indicates the opportunity for increasing the utility of such a concept by making available to the designer at the terminal *all* of the computer programs he needs. COGO, and even STRESS, are fine in their own right, he maintains, but are limited to portions of the total problem facing the civil engineer. Roos describes an example: "Even in a relatively small problem, such as the design of a highway interchange, the engineer must

[2] *IBM Computing Report*, Vol. I, No. 3, December 1965, p. 12.

consider the highway location and safety (highway engineering), settlement, stability and foundation conditions (soil engineering), and traffic flow (transportation engineering)."[3]

Roos and his associates, under the direction of Professor C. L. Miller, are working to construct an integrated civil engineering system termed ICES which will allow a civil engineer to use all of these disciplines together—that is, without having to separate them into individual tasks, work on them separately, and later integrate the results. Roos envisions a system which permits the engineer to sit down at the terminal and consider all parts of the problem, working between them as necessary, and having results transferred between disciplines as they are calculated. Significant problems of data management and dynamic memory allocation must be overcome to achieve the desired system. Nevertheless, this work is significant as a recognition of the need for the engineer to deal with the whole problem and of the computer's capability for assisting in the coordinating task.

APPLICATIONS TO ANALYSIS

Thus far, in this chapter, we have described the manner in which the computer has been brought into the engineering design process. We have been focusing on the developments in language and computer operation that have progressively improved the communication between the engineer and the machine. We have observed the development of higher-level language, problem-oriented language, and real-time operation. Real-time operation on a useful and meaningful scale is a recent development. We will have more to say about it later. Now, we'd like to turn our attention to the design problems that have been put on the computer. Whatever the drawbacks of language and availability, major applications have been programmed and significant savings in time and cost have been achieved.

Undertaking an analysis application is a larger task than simple computation. Analysis requires that the concept for the design be developed in sufficient detail to permit the construction of a conceptual model. Such a model reflects the pertinent physical principles and can be used to predict performance under varying conditions.

Because most companies approach design problems in their own way, most analysis applications have been too specialized to be of general value.

[3] Roos, *op. cit.,* p. 8.

This is not to say that they could not have been made general purpose, had that been a requirement. Rather, it reflects the fact that it is cheaper and easier to develop special-purpose analysis programs.

The aerospace companies have, over the years, developed significant analysis applications. O. D. Smith, Computing Technology Department, Los Angeles Division of North American Aviation, described to us a program which analyzes aircraft engine performance. Engineers can input engine parameters in any combination and receive as output detailed performance measurements for the design in question. Such an analysis program allows the engineer to try various combinations of design parameters before committing his design to paper.

The Boeing Company in Seattle has developed programs for analysis of the structural dynamics of aircraft and space designs. Flutter and vibration resulting from airframe design must be examined in detail as early in the design process as possible. The structural-dynamics computer programs permit this to be done at an early stage. William Fetter, Supervisor of Computer Graphics at Boeing, stated that the information derived from these structural-dynamics analyses when displayed graphically can help in defining the structural arrangement such as optimal placement of engine mountings on an aircraft wing or fuselage. This can be an aid to essential wind-tunnel tests.

The Metal Structures Corporation of Grapevine, Texas, has written an analysis program for designing metal buildings. The engineer is able to:

> (1) enter into the computer the loading specifications of the proposed frame metal building and the preliminary design he believes will meet them, and (2) receive back from the computer a report showing the forces the proposed design will withstand compared to actual forces resulting from the loading specification—with differences and percentage of variance shown, as well as material and fabrication costs.[4]

The engineer can go through the process for as many iterations as he needs in order to get the balance he wants in style, weight, and cost.

At the Ford Motor Company, work is currently being done under William Hogue of the Body Engineering Department on the analysis of windshield wiper mechanisms. The shape of the windshield is determined by styling considerations. The Body Engineering Department is responsible for designing a wiper mechanism that will meet design and visual standards while not causing excessive distortion of the wiper blade. Variables include the placement of the pivot point and the length of the

4 *IBM Computing Report, op. cit.,* p. 6.

wiper blade. Present analysis methods include a computer program which simulates the movement of the blade incrementally across the surface and outputs data representing the area cleared during the simulated blade motion across the windshield surface. Changing the pivot point and blade length permits the designer to iterate to an acceptable final design.

Another analysis application at Ford is concerned with the optical distortion resulting from a given windshield design. In order to determine the amount and severity of the distortion, it was heretofore necessary to construct a prototype windshield. By placing a reference grid on one side and a camera on the other an exposure was made. The windshield was removed and another exposure was made. The resulting photographs, when compared, specified the distortion caused by the windshield configuration. The computer program operates with a mathematical definition of the inner and outer surfaces of the windshield. The space coordinates of the driver's eye and a set of points representing the grid are input data. The analysis program constructs lines from the driver's eye, through the windshield (accounting for the angle of incidence, the angles of refraction, and the index of refraction of glass) to the grid points. Comparing the virtual image thus created with the undistorted reference grid points provides a measure of the distortion. The two methods are shown in Exhibits 2A and 2B.

A set of problems, which we have seen occurring in the design process, is found in the integrating and coordinating of individual design efforts to avoid interference and to ensure that components, when assembled, will function together to fulfill the performance requirements for the system.

An example of the interference problem was explained to us by William Hogue at Ford. In designing a window regulator mechanism, it is necessary to raise and lower the glass following a predetermined path. The location of pivots and the length of the arms determine the path the glass follows. The computer program will generate a set of values indicating where key elements can be located and the length of the bars. Thus potential interferences can be reduced.

AUTOMATED DESIGN

We have been concerning ourselves with the manner in which the computer has been called on to assist the engineer in design. We have implied that man has a role in the process. Indeed, in our opinion, he

ANALYSIS OF OPTICAL DISTORTION IN AUTOMOBILE WINDSHIELD

Manual method:

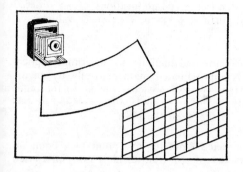

• The test windshield is placed between a standard grid plane and a stationary camera positioned at the driver's eye point. An exposure is made of the grid plane with the windshield in position.

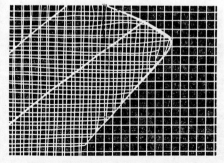

• The windshield is then removed and a second exposure is made of the grid.

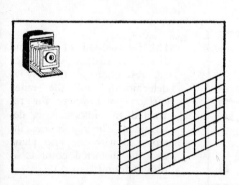

• The resultant double exposure shows both the distorted and undistorted grid patterns.

Source: Ford Motor Company, W. Hogue, Design and Drafting Services, Metal Stamping Division.

EXHIBIT 2A

ANALYSIS OF OPTICAL DISTORTION IN AUTOMOBILE WINDSHIELD

Computer method:

Input to the computer program consists of point locations of an ordered set of points on the test windshield surface, eyepoint coordinate values, and grid surface point locations.

The computer performs the following calculations to determine optical distortion. The windshield surface is approximated mathematically by an array of bi-cubic surface patches. Surface normals are constructed on the outer surface, and an ordered set of points on the inner surface is generated by offsetting along surface normals by the thickness of the glass.

Next, a line or ray trace is constructed from the eye point to a point on the grid plane. The mathematical model of the windshield is now interposed between the grid and the eye point.

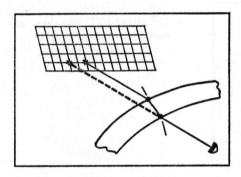

• The intersection of the line and inner surface is calculated, refraction of the ray is determined, and the outer surface point where the refracted ray intersects is determined. The ray is then intersected with the grid plane and the distorted point location is found.

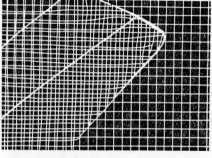

• By repeating the procedure for each point on the grid, the computer generated a set of points comprising the distorted grid. A drawing of the distorted grids is made using a numerically controlled drafting machine.

Source: Ford Motor Company, W. Hogue, Design and Drafting Services, Metal Stamping Division.

EXHIBIT 2B

always will. But his role will be greatly changed. An example, in the extreme, of the designer being displaced by the computer is the IBM-developed Automated Design Engineering (ADE) system in use at the ITE Circuit Breaker Company in Philadelphia. Used for the first time in late 1963, this system produces detailed design specifications for transformers.

Program input consists of customer specifications for coiling media, KVA, voltages, impedance, cycle, physical characteristics, and options. The process is described as follows:

> . . . the system proceeds to electrical design on the assumption a standard core is to be used. Values for core characteristics are assigned and the low and high voltage coils are designed consecutively. Each coil design is iterated first for wire size, then for temperature rise; current density is changed until temperature rise falls within required limits; in this example, less than 150 degrees. Next, impedance and total copper losses are computed. If either falls outside allowable tolerances, certain design parameters such as current density and impedance gap are changed, and the windings are redesigned. Dimensional clearance between coils is then calculated and checked against minimum required clearance. Where it does not fit, a new core must be designed and the entire process repeated until temperature rise, impedance, copper losses, and clearance are fully satisfactory. In a final step, dimensions and winding characteristics are computed for core and coil.[5]

The program prints out detailed instructions for fabrication and assembly of these electrical parts of the transformer. It then proceeds to the mechanical design, ending again with a bill of materials and assembly plans.

Note the manner in which the designs for elements are formulated, tested for performance and made to fit with the rest of the system, and then kept or rejected. It was possible in this case to completely specify the design process, even though it was iterative. The totally structured nature of the process permitted the computer to assume the whole task.

It is perfectly appropriate and desirable to use the computer for engineering design to whatever extent is possible and economically justifiable. In the ITE case, transformer design had been reduced to a clerical chore and was, therefore, programmable. Thirty minutes of time on an IBM 1401 and one day of processing replaced the previous processing time of six days or more. Our concern in this report is not for such systems. We are concerned with the design process in general, and not with those isolated instances which are so highly structured as not to require human judgment, intuition, and creativity.

[5] Holstein, David, "Automated Design Engineering," *Datamation*, June 1964.

THE COMPUTER IN DESIGN

The computer is useful in the design process because it is capable of performing large amounts of computation. More importantly, it is useful because the process of analysis normally includes conceptual models which may be programmable. By simulating the performance of the design, it is possible to predict the degree to which the design satisfies the specifications established for it.

In bringing the power of the computer to bear on design problems, the engineer has been faced with obstacles in effectively communicating with it, and in gaining access to it, on a meaningful basis. Language development and new concepts of computer operations have substantially reduced the obstacles. Despite the obstacles, engineers have developed extensive programs to assist in analysis. We have mentioned a very few examples. In some cases, a great deal, or all, of the design process can be automated. The designer, however, will continue to play the major role in most design processes for the foreseeable future. In most processes he performs functions that can never be displaced by a machine incapable of judgment, overcoming ambiguity or expressing esthetic values.

CHAPTER IV

THE ROLE OF PASSIVE
COMPUTER GRAPHICS •

WE HAVE DISCUSSED the design process at some length, and we have examined the evolution of computer assistance to design. We are now ready to consider the impact computer graphics has had on design. Our first step will be to hypothesize an ideal design system and indicate the role "passive" computer graphics plays in such a system.

AN IDEAL DESIGN SYSTEM

The ideal engineering design system is one that recognizes the respective attributes of the two partners: the man and the computer. We have previously noted the computer's speed, memory, and reliability. We must now account for the man's attributes.

The designer brings to the design problem his experience, imagination, social and esthetic values, and a tolerance for ambiguity. By experience we don't mean just an accumulation of technical tools: we mean much more. He brings a massive bank of information about the world, about design, about relationships and associations. On the basis of this experience, and in conjunction with his imaginative powers, he can be creative, innovative, or inventive.

Henry Dreyfuss, the Industrial Designer, has described the process he goes through in preparation for developing a new design. He first tries to become saturated with information about the product, its users, the available materials, the utility aspects of the item, safety considerations, and anything else that is relevant. He examines competitive products, reads, talks to engineers, talks to salesmen. When he is ready, he turns his thoughts to the new design. He imagines new shapes, new arrangements, new configurations. Scratching on paper with pencil serves to record the process. At first in broad outline, and then in more and more detail, the design takes shape. This ability to create is unique to man.

The designer is able to include, in his judgment of alternative designs, his social and esthetic values. The precise curve of an automobile roof may never have existed before. From among the endless alternative shapes that are possible, the designer selects one because it pleases him. The selection is on no basis that is quantifiable. It cannot be programmed.

We noted in Chapter III, while discussing the ITE system for transformer design, that that particular process was fully determinable. This is not the general case. Normally, stages in the design process are reached when the physical principles and quantitative tools at the engineer's disposal will not suffice to determine a design or range of alternative designs which will perform as required. In the face of inadequate data, the designer is capable of proceeding. He may later reverse his decision as more data become available, but he can make a decision and proceed on the basis of it. He is capable of intuition and hunch. He can formulate unforeseen questions that arise during the process and that could not have been anticipated.

An ideal engineering design system will take into account the respective attributes of the participants. What the machine can do better, it will do. What the man can do better, he will do. As the process becomes better known, the documentable portions can be turned over to the machine.

The system must be interactive, as judged from the man's point of view. When the man needs the computer's assistance, it should be available. The process of brief, unpredictable creative moments interspersed with lengthy periods of analysis must give way to a process wherein the analysis time is steadily reduced, approaching zero. Should the analysis be lengthy, even though done by the computer, the man must be able to monitor the progress and intervene if he observes no meaningful results forthcoming. For this reason the computer must keep the designer apprised of its progress.

The communication between man and computer must be in a language natural to the man. The system must be capable of graphic communication as well as by way of the traditional symbol string.

The response of the computer system must be determined by the man's reaction time and tolerance for delay. The designer should feel that progress with the design problem is governed by his own ability to proceed, not that of the machine.

The computer must make available a file of the pertinent standard information to be accessed as needed in the process of developing the design. Standard parts, characteristics of materials, production standards —all must be immediately available to be used as required.

The system must be so organized that it serves to record the progress of the design. It must include a retrievable record of all aspects of the project. The latest version of the design for each element, each component, and the entire system must be on call. Changes made by any engineer should be automatically reflected in other affected designs. If the change cannot be automatically made, an indication of the need for attention by the engineer should be set. The designer should be able to simulate the operation of his design in conjunction with associated designs in order to detect interferences and determine performance.

Finally, the specification of the solution should be largely an automatic process. The generation of hard-copy output, manufacturing specifications, and numerical control tapes should proceed when signaled.

Clearly, computer graphics plays a large part in the ideal system. Graphics is the language of design; and, if the engineer is to be relieved of the need to recast his thoughts into an unnatural form, graphics must be part of the communication process. Further, graphics permits the flow of large amounts of information between the engineer and the computer at a useful rate. Rather than receive a three-inch pile of printer output six hours after submitting the run, the engineer can view a family of curves in minutes, if not seconds. Rather than specify that every conceivable permutation of the parameters for an analysis be tried, he can try a few, view the response, decide quickly the relevant range, and iterate to a solution in short order. Rather than be forced to build a model in order to view a shape that is difficult to imagine from orthographic views, he can cause a view to rotate on the screen, thus getting a feel for the shape. This isn't to say that models will be eliminated. Rather, they will be made only when it is desirable, as some designer's have suggested to us, to be able to feel the esthetic shape, or when certain performance tests or characteristics have not given way to simulation.

PASSIVE COMPUTER GRAPHICS, EQUIPMENT AND APPLICATIONS

We indicated earlier that computer graphics is a broad term, which includes many ingenious devices and applications outside of, as well as within, the engineering design function. A case in point would be the American Airlines SABRE system for airline reservations. Our concern, of course, is for the emerging uses of computer graphics *within* the design process. We have found that it is useful to make a further distinction between "passive" and "active" computer graphics.

Passive computer graphics includes the capability for communicating graphical information to or from the computer in an off-line or non-real-time manner. The hardware devices associated with this kind of use include a variety of image recorders and scanners, cathode ray tube displays, and digital plotters. An example of this equipment appears in Exhibit 1. Some equipment scans drawings on paper and converts them, through a micro-film medium, to digital form for computer storage. The General Motors DAC-I (Design Augmented by Computer) system includes such a device. Such equipment still has limitations—that is, the conversion is not entirely automatic. Consider, for example, the problem of representing, in computer storage, the figure "8" as normally written by hand (one smooth line). In order to be useful it must be manipulated as a single entity, but it is difficult to design a scanning system that will recognize the figure as a single entity and not as two juxtaposed closed loops. The problem arises because sometimes we *want* two juxtaposed closed loops, and the figure may not be a figure "8" at all. Currently such difficulties are overcome by accomplishing the scanning under program control so that a man can intervene and avoid incorrect interpretations.

Digital plotters have been developed in a variety of sizes and with a variety of capabilities. Some are the size of a briefcase, while others fill a normal-sized room. Some are meant to produce gross representations, while others are accurate to within a thousandth of an inch. The larger, more accurate plotters have been used for some time by the aerospace industry, for example, to produce full-scale drawings. Such plotters generally are driven by an electronic control unit, which reads a magnetic or punched tape and performs the digital-to-analog conversion. Plotting speed is too slow for direct, on-line connection to a computer.

One piece of equipment that has been put to very imaginative use is the Stromberg Carlson 4020. This device also operates as an off-line unit, accepting as input magnetic tape prepared by the computer. The function

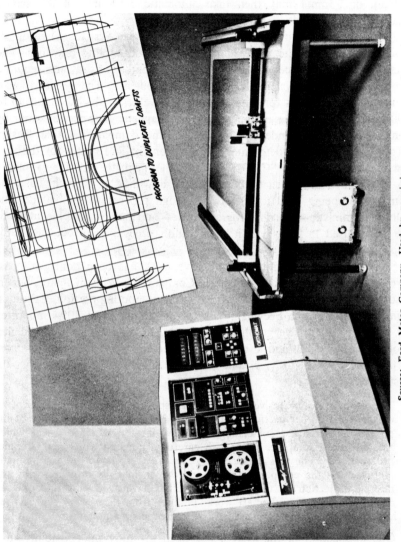

ORTHOMAT PLOTTER

PROGRAM TO DUPLICATE DRAFTS

Source: Ford Motor Company. Used by permission.

EXHIBIT 1

of the SC 4020 is to take graphic images that are on the tape in digital form and convert them into displays on a cathode ray tube. A camera (16mm or 35mm) may then take automatic exposures of the screen images, and the result is images on a roll of film.

A useful application at the Missile and Space Systems Division of Douglas Aircraft is the production of wiring and cabling drawings. The usefulness of this device is apparent when the number of drawings required for advanced space systems is realized. At Douglas, "The system is now being used on projects for the Saturn launch vehicles which contain up to 8000 cables."[1] The file of images on the magnetic tape is generated by computer programs under the control of the company's Cable Design Group. The programs determine optimum lengths and routes for the wiring and harnesses. The SC 4020 converts the magnetic tape file to images on film, which may then be converted to drawings as needed. Thus the computer is being used to perform a design process which had become fully deterministic—that is, programmable—and passive graphic methods are being used in the solution specification process by producing hardcopy documentation.

Some particularly unique and creative work has been done with passive graphic techniques at The Boeing Company by William Fetter, Supervisor of Computer Graphics. The basis of the computing portion of this system, directed by John Freyman, is at this writing an IBM 7094 supported by a variety of passive graphic equipment including an Orthomat digital plotter, an SC 4020, and a Telereader (used for transcribing points from orthographic views to x, y, and z coordinates). As Fetter describes the system:

> The tedious and expensive process of transposing orthographic views of an object into true perspective illustrations is reduced to the translation of the points of reference from orthographic drawings to punched cards, which are fed into a computer along with carefully prepared Computer Graphics programming. The true perspective views are then drawn by an automatic plotter using the computer output, and the engineer is provided with any desired projection or view of the object as a finished drawing or as an accurate basis for further art work. Pictures from the system can be used in still, stereo, motion picture, and oscilloscope presentations.[2]

One application of the system has been to study pilot visibility in a

[1] "Computer Designs Missile Cables," *Steel,* May 10, 1965, p. 81.
[2] Fetter, William A., "Computer Graphics in Engineering Communication," a presentation to the 1963 Engineering Institute on Design and Drafting Automation, University of Wisconsin.

variety of aircraft. The object is to determine what can or cannot be seen by the pilot as he looks out from the cockpit during a number of maneuvers. For example, a sequence was produced accurately depicting the pilot's view of an aircraft carrier landing. Orthographic views of the carrier were obtained and simplified to show only the lines of the hull, flight deck, and island that were of interest. By converting these views to x, y, and z coordinates using a Telereader, and processing them on the 7094, views were produced as seen from various distances during the approach and at touchdown. On these views were superimposed cockpit masks so as to depict only what was visible from the pilot's position. The result is a sequence that can be studied by designers and pilots to determine the visibility of important regions of the carrier during the landing. A movie was prepared by a similar process for added realism. A sequence of selected frames is shown in Exhibit 2.

The masking can be modified to show the view with one eye or with both eyes. The pilot's head can be held stationary, swivelled, or moved backward and forward. The view can be modified to reflect upper body movements.

Similar sequences and movies have been produced to show night and day landings at the Seattle-Tacoma airport. Landing sequences show the runway, horizon, and buildings changing perspective view. The scene moves to reflect the aircraft's change of attitude to the appropriate one for landing, including the plane's suspension system absorbing the impact of landing.

To appreciate fully the significance of Fetter's work, it should be realized that these pictures are true perspective views arrived at in a precise manner. They represent reality as nearly as a simulation can, based on the requirement and the budget. Further, when these sequences were produced, the aircraft in question had not been constructed, let alone flown. Simulations of existing aircraft have also been prepared on the computer, viewed by pilots who have flown the aircraft, and endorsed for their accuracy. The value of such tools to designers is immense.

In another application of his passive computer graphics technology, Fetter produced a Support Systems motion picture depicting a maintenance crew removing the jet engine from a single-engine fighter aircraft. The crew of men are shown removing panels from the rear of the aircraft, maneuvering an engine-handling dolly under the plane, raising the carriage to support the engine, removing engine mounting bolts, lowering the engine in such a manner as to clear the aircraft, and maneuvering the dolly carry-

PILOT VISIBILITY

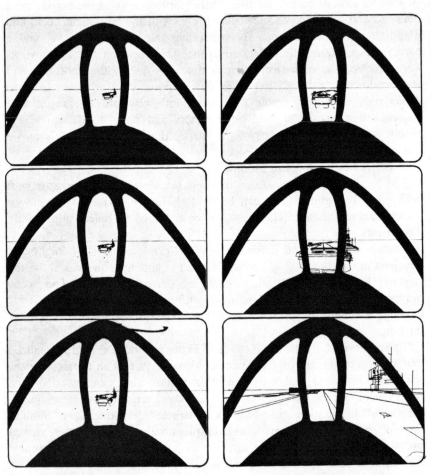

(Sequence of pilot views of landing on a CVA-59 carrier showing cockpit mask)
Source: William Fetter and John Freyman. Permission of The Boeing Company.

EXHIBIT 2

ing the engine away from the plane. During the sequence a clock appears which indicates elapsed time to certain points in the process. With this pictorial version of the process to study, designers can consider changes to speed up, or in other ways improve, the procedure. Such assistance in visualizing a complex process can contribute significantly to avoiding troublesome interference problems, which, when discovered early in the design process, are far less costly to correct.

Passive computer graphics at Boeing is assisting senior designers in analyzing certain performance characteristics for a design. It is assisting in keeping management informed of the latest concepts. It is being used to document some design specifications. It is being used to support proposal presentations for defense contracts. Some powerful tools, and a great deal of imagination, are contributing to the design process and the public relations aspects of an engineering-oriented company.

North American Aviation has developed a passive graphics system called AUTODRAFT, which assists in the design documentation process. The designer, having arrived at the solution to his design problem, prepares a layout depicting the individual parts, their size, shape, and relation to each other. From this point, a designer-draftsman uses the computer system and a variety of off-line optical and digital plotters to produce detail drawings of the individual parts and an assembly drawing. The output might be a precision template, provided the draftsman chose a high-precision plotter for the output device. The system makes use of a drafting language—that is, the designer-draftsman encodes the information from the layout in the AUTODRAFT language to be subsequently keypunched and input to the computer. A major benefit of this system was described as follows: "A point of vital importance is that the system can be used to capture, within the computer, production design information at its point of origin—the detailer—thus minimizing such problems as transcription errors and clerical errors."[3]

We would be remiss, in discussing the use of passive graphics in the design process, if we did not describe the work currently being done by the consulting firm of Arthur D. Little for the U.S. Navy, Bureau of Ships. Under the direction of Dr. Bernhard Romberg, a computer system for carrying out the detailed design of the structure of surface naval ships is in preparation.

The ship design process traditionally consists of three stages. In the

[3] Harris, Herbert R., and O. Dale Smith, "AUTODRAFT—A Language and Processor for Design and Drafting," a presentation to the SHARE-Design Automation Workshop, Atlantic City, New Jersey, June 24, 1965.

preliminary design stage the task is specified in terms of parameters for performance. The desired range, crew, speed, size, and rough cost are established. During the contract design stage major systems are defined; and the major structural members, machinery, electrical, piping, and weapons systems are positioned. The configuration of each part, and such questions as the manner of intersection of structural members, are resolved during the detailed design phase. The output of this last step includes detailed drawings and templates prepared on plotters. The Navy's new system will perform the detailed design function for ship structure and provide the graphic construction aids for use in cutting and assembling and programs which can be further processed to produce control tapes for numerically controlled fabricating equipment.

This system is a major undertaking. It draws on catalogs of standards concerning materials and design, lofting, and construction procedures and knowledge. It will be used by naval architects to prepare complete construction packages for shipyards. The system is one part of an overall Navy plan for computerizing ship design, including hull design which is done at the contract design stage. This overall plan is under the direction of Commander Donald Craig, U.S. Navy, Ship Systems Command.

THE ROLE OF PASSIVE GRAPHICS IN THE IDEAL SYSTEM

Recalling our earlier discussion of an ideal design system, we can list the system requirements as follows:
- It will take into account the respective capabilities of the man and the machine.
- It will provide for the passing to the machine of those functions of design that become deterministic and programmable.
- The system will include the ability to be interactive from the engineer's point of view, providing rapid response and the option for the engineer to intervene to halt pointless computer operation.
- The communication between man and machine must be by graphics in addition to symbol strings.
- The computer will provide standards information as required.
- The computer will maintain a complete record of the design as it progresses, accessible to the man.
- The system will provide for the reflection of changes in associated elements of the design.
- The system will provide for the detection of interferences and the determination of performance through simulation.

- The specification of the solution will be largely an automatic process.

Passive computer graphics has had its greatest impact in satisfying the last two requirements. William Fetter's work has shown the value of passive graphic techniques in detecting interferences. Evaluating performance is exemplified by his pilot vision studies. The work at Douglas Aircraft in cable design, the North American AUTODRAFT system, and the Navy Bureau of Ships detailed design system exemplify the feasibility and the value of passive graphic techniques in design solution specification.

CHAPTER V

THE ROLE OF ACTIVE
COMPUTER GRAPHICS •

ACTIVE COMPUTER GRAPHICS is characterized by real-time operation. In such a system man-machine communication is highly interactive as well as graphical. The relationship between the designer and the computer is intimate, and progress is paced by the designer. The computer responds to a problem posed in graphical and nongraphical terms with a reply couched in the same terms. Clearly, the major role to be played by active computer graphics is in assisting the designer to conceptualize and analyze his design. Additionally, it will prove useful for design solution specification.

CONSOLE EQUIPMENT

The basic active graphics hardware is typically grouped into a console. As shown in Exhibit 1, the equipment usually includes a cathode ray tube, a light pen or voltage pencil, a "function" keyboard, and an alphanumeric keyboard. Graphic input is accomplished by drawing on the scope face with the light pen or voltage pencil. Graphic output is by display on the scope. Nongraphic communication is accomplished by use of the alphanumeric keyboard. The operator typically directs the process by use of the function keyboard and by indicating areas of interest on the display with the light pen or voltage pencil. For example, with the light pen pointed at one spot on the screen, the operator might press the function button

A GENERAL COMPUTER GRAPHICS SYSTEM

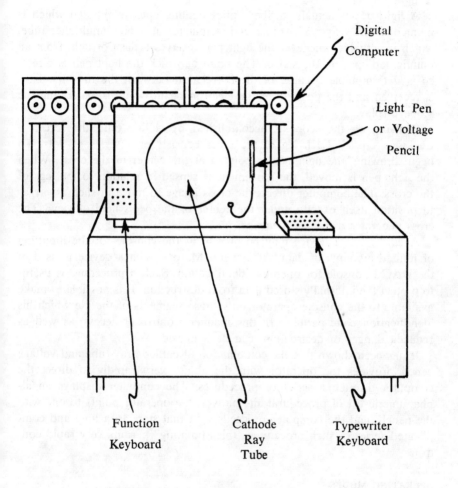

Digital
Computer

Light Pen
or Voltage
Pencil

Function
Keyboard

Cathode
Ray
Tube

Typewriter
Keyboard

EXHIBIT 1

"Straight line begin." The pen would be moved across the screen to the desired termination point and the "Line end" button would be pressed. If desired, the computer would ensure that the line is geometrically straight.

A light pen is actually a fiber optics bundle, open at the end which is pointed at the scope. The other end terminates at a photomultiplier tube, which is actuated whenever the light pen receives a flash of light from an illuminated spot on the scope. The point at which the light pen is directed is determinable because of the correlation between the time the flash is received and the position of the electron beam which is generating the scope display.

Drawing on the scope is accomplished by calling onto the screen a tracking "cross." Each leg of the cross consists of a series of dots. To begin drawing, the light pen is pointed at the center of the cross. When the light pen is moved, the movement is sensed in relation to the legs of the cross. The computer directs the cross image to move in such a way as to position itself exactly under the center of the pen's field of view. The cross generates a line as it moves.

A card-reading device may be present at the console for the inputting of limited amounts of data. At General Motors, such a device is used at the DAC-I console for operator identification. Such a procedure is useful to protect the internally stored data from destruction. It is possible to make available to the console operator only those segments of the file which his identification code permits. In this manner, control of access, as well as reduced danger of destruction, can be achieved.

It has been shown that the combination of cathode ray tube and voltage pencil provides the operator with the ability very rapidly to direct the computer through a series of procedures. The computer displays an alphanumeric list of procedural alternatives, the operator points to one with the pencil, and the computer proceeds with that step. In a long and complicated series of such procedures, this "pointing" permits very rapid control.

OPERATING MODES

Consoles, such as we've described, can be connected on-line with the computer in any one of three operating modes. One is on a full-time basis; that is, while in operation the console is the only device being serviced by the computer. This method has been typical of some development configurations. In Lockheed-Georgia's configuration (see Exhibit 2), for

LOCKHEED-GEORGIA COMPUTER GRAPHIC CONFIGURATION

UNIVAC 418 Computer

DIGITAL EQUIPMENT CORP.
TYPE 340 Display

| 418 to 340 INTER FACE | UNIVAC 418 CENTRAL PROCESSOR | CARD READER PRINTER |
| DEC 340 DISPLAY | FUNCTION SELECTION CONSOLE | MAG- NETIC TAPE UNITS |

Source: *Lockheed-Georgia Quarterly,* Summer 1965.

EXHIBIT 2

example, a Digital Equipment Corporation Model 340 display has been interfaced with a Univac 418 central processor on a full-time basis.

The second operating mode is on a multiprogramming basis. This scheme, as described in Chapter III, includes the provision for the central processor to operate in the traditional batch mode and serve the console in real-time on an interrupt basis. An example of such a configuration is General Motors' DAC-I system. As shown in Exhibits 3A and 3B, a specially designed and constructed console is serviced by an IBM 7094 specially augmented with an extra 32K words of memory.

The third operating mode is time-sharing. Under this scheme, the computer services many users, while giving each the impression he has full use of the computer. At this time, active computer graphics consoles have not been operated under time-sharing to the best of our knowledge. Such a scheme is necessary, however, for the full benefits of a graphics system to be achieved, not only because of the economics of central processor usage, but also because of the necessity to provide real-time, interactive service to a large number of designers in most organizations.[1]

The amount of central processor time required to service a console has been appreciably reduced by the development of special console-support hardware. The rationale for this development is the fact that for most of the time that a user is operating at a console nothing new is happening. The designer is studying the display, or referencing some notes, or reaching for the light pen. The display, however, must be regenerated many times a second. If the central processor were tied up maintaining the image, it would be unavailable to do much else. By putting display maintenance circuitry at the console, the central processor is freed for other work.

This raises the issue of just what kind of overall hardware configuration is desirable for an operational active computer graphics system. Since no such system presently exists, we can only point out that the answer will be determined largely by what kinds of capabilities are required. Some people have suggested that a number of consoles may be supported by a buffer unit, such as the one described above for display maintenance. Processing would be performed on a large computer which was servicing several such sets of consoles (see Exhibit 4A). Others suggest that the

[1] As this book was being prepared for publication (May 1966), we were notified by Lockheed-Georgia that it had installed a Control Data 3300 computer with three consoles, associated tape drives, and disk file. This system was being checked out using both time-sharing and application programs written by the Lockheed-Georgia staff. They anticipated that this would be the first time-shared graphics system and the first production use of computer-aided design in the aerospace industry.

GENERAL MOTORS CORPORATION DAC-I, DESIGN AUGMENTED BY COMPUTERS

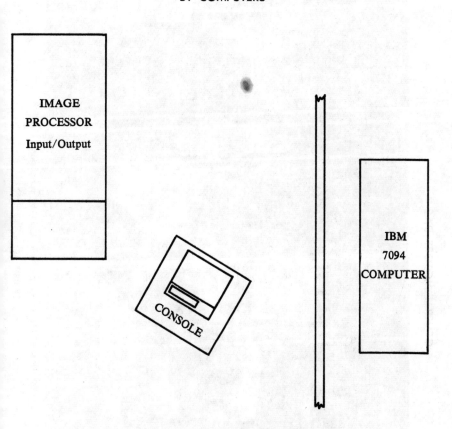

(IBM 7960 Special Image Processing System, designed and built by IBM according to General Motors specifications)

EXHIBIT 3A

GENERAL MOTORS DAC-I

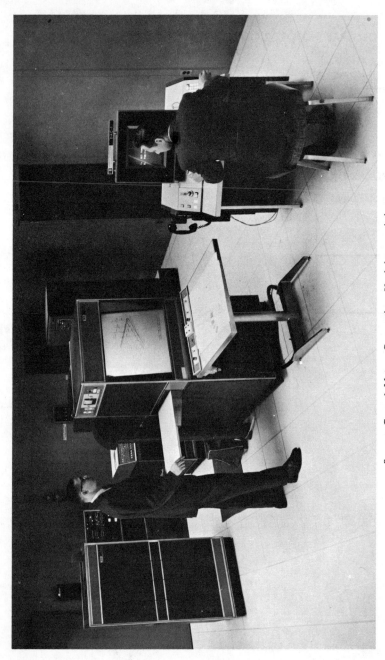

Source: General Motors Corporation. Used by permission.

EXHIBIT 3B

HARDWARE CONFIGURATION FOR COMPUTER GRAPHICS

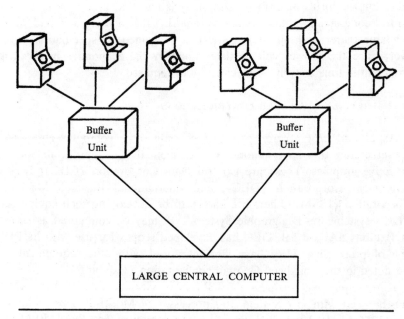

A.

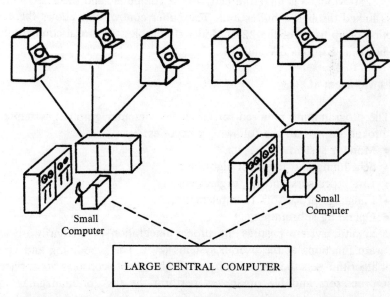

B.

EXHIBIT 4

consoles be additionally supported by a small local computer for the more limited forms of drawing and analysis and that access be to a large central computer for those functions requiring the memory size and speed available there (Exhibit 4B). Little can be gained by speculation, however, since the answer will be determined by the economics involved at any point in time as well as the capabilities required.

COMMERCIALLY AVAILABLE CONFIGURATIONS

As of mid-1966, there appear to be only three computer equipment manufacturers that have announced equipment that is appropriate for use in active graphics. These are Control Data Corporation (CDC), Digital Equipment Corporation (DEC), and International Business Machines Corporation (IBM). Others are known to be developing such equipment. CDC's system, the Digigraphic System 270, may be configured as shown in Exhibits 5A and 5B. DEC has developed scopes for use with its PDP line of processors. They have also interfaced with other equipment, as we noted in the Lockheed-Georgia configuration (Exhibit 2).

IBM's equipment includes the IBM 2250 Graphic Display Unit which can be used with any System 360 processor of Model-30 size or larger. The 2250 Model I is linked directly to the computer, and the 2250 Model II is linked through a buffer unit. The buffer control unit allows the connection of up to six of the 2250 Model II consoles. A partial configuration is shown in Exhibits 6A and 6B.

SOFTWARE PROBLEMS

The programming required for an active computer graphics system can be broken down into the following categories:
- Monitor system.
- Scheduling and interrupt algorithm.
- List processors and file organizers.
- Language processors (compilers).
- Operating subroutines.

The monitor system ensures the proper integration of all hardware and software functions at the overall systems level. The scheduling and interrupt algorithm sets the timetable by which the remote consoles are serviced. List processors and file organizers perform the task of managing large masses of data; storing it as received from a console, retrieving and ma-

CONTROL DATA CORPORATION DIGIGRAPHIC 270 SYSTEM

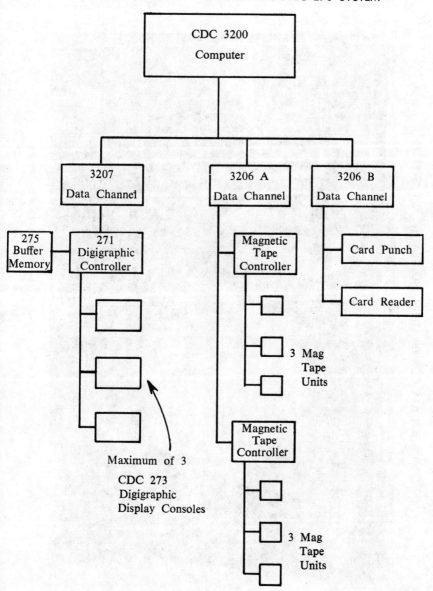

Source: CDC Digigraphic System 270 Function Control Program Specifications Handbook.

EXHIBIT 5A

CONTROL DATA CORPORATION DIGIGRAPHIC 270 SYSTEM

Source: Control Data Corporation, Burlington, Massachusetts. Used by permission.

EXHIBIT 5B

IBM 2250 DISPLAY SYSTEM

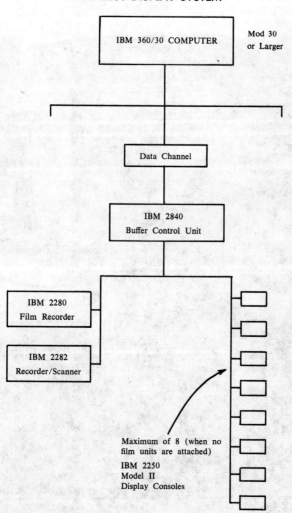

Source: Interview with Dr. Frank Skinner, IBM System Development Laboratory, Kingston, New York.

EXHIBIT 6A

IBM 2250 GRAPHIC DATA PROCESSING SYSTEM

Source: IBM System Development Laboratory, Kingston, New York. Used by permission.

EXHIBIT 6B

nipulating it as required by all parts of the system. Language processors, also known as compilers, accept programs and translate them into machine language for execution. Operating subroutines include the programs that have been prepared to perform specific kinds of computation, analyses, and image-processing duties.

The software problems associated with an operating active graphics facility are immense. They result from three primary factors. First, a fully developed graphics facility presupposes a time-sharing system. The problems associated with servicing a large number of remote terminals, each of which requires the availability of its own data and operating subroutines, in such a manner as to give the illusion of full-time service have not been fully overcome. Second, while it is relatively easy to provide the designer with the ability to draw on the scope, and then manipulate his drawing as a *drawing*, it is a far greater task to communicate graphically with a designer about an object with its associated geometry, properties, linkages, and identification. Substantial advances in graphic communication are required to overcome this problem. Third, the techniques required to organize and manage a bank of data so as to reflect all these aspects of an object, and to facilitate the performance of a wide variety of analyses in an efficient manner, are not yet fully developed. Oscar Hefner of Lockheed-Georgia put it as follows:

> A relatively simple description can provide the capability of creating a picture of the design and allow the designer to manipulate this picture as if he were drafting it. The description becomes quite complex, and is not nearly so well defined, when the requirement is to allow the designer to request that virtually any calculation such as stress analysis, weight analysis, volume, and surface area be made upon his design.[2]

This is not to say that the problems are insurmountable. Indeed, advances are being made regularly. A number of people at the Massachusetts Institute of Technology are currently addressing the problems. They include Dr. Lawrence Roberts, Douglas T. Ross, and Timothy Johnson.

SOME HISTORY OF ACTIVE COMPUTER GRAPHICS

It is not our purpose here to record a definitive history of the development of active computer graphics. Nevertheless, perspective can be gained by mentioning some of the important user developments.

[2] Hefner, Oscar, "Systems Programming for Graphics," *Lockheed-Georgia Quarterly*, Summer 1965, p. 12.

The General Motors DAC project grew from a study begun in the late 1950's to determine the potential role of computers in the graphical phases of design. Early investigations demonstrated the feasibility of scanning and digitizing lines on film, and of manipulating three dimensional images by computer. As Edwin L. Jacks reported to the 1964 Fall Joint Computer Conference:

> The initial goal of the DAC-I project was the development of a combination of computer hardware and software which (a) would permit "conversational" man-machine graphical communication and (b) would provide a maximum programming flexibility and ease of use for experimentation. This goal was achieved in early 1963. . . . From the standpoint of a laboratory facility, the system is performing excellently. We are learning that man and machine can communicate readily via graphical means.[3]

The DAC-I system has been in operation eight hours a day since 1963. This installation has accumulated more operational experience than any other.

Ivan Sutherland is generally credited with the pioneering effort in demonstrating the feasibility of useful graphical communication using a cathode ray tube, light pen, and function-keyboard console. His work done during the period 1960 to 1962 on the M.I.T. TX-2 computer has become recognized as a classic under the name SKETCHPAD. Exhibit 7 is a sketch of Sutherland at the TX-2 console.

On the basis of these pioneering efforts, and the continuing work being done at M.I.T., the Lockheed-Georgia Company began a development effort in late 1963. M. D. Prince, now associate director of research, Systems Sciences, was introduced to active computer graphics through the industrial liaison program at M.I.T. From an initial study in early 1964, Lockheed-Georgia selected hardware and was operational for research purposes by the end of 1964. By mid-1965 a wide variety of functions has been programmed. As reported by S. H. Chasen,

> The capabilities that exist to date (mid-1965) on the C.A.D. system include the following features:
> - Four views: three principal projections and, optionally, either an isometric or perspective.
> - Conversion to display any desired view and return to four views on request.
> - Definition of points.

[3] Jacks, Edwin L., "A Laboratory for the Study of Graphical Man-Machine Communication," *Proceedings—Fall Joint Computer Conference, 1964*, Spartan Books, Inc., Baltimore, 1964.

THE SKETCHPAD CONSOLE ON THE TX-2 COMPUTER AT
LINCOLN LABORATORY, M.I.T.

Source: *McGraw-Hill Yearbook of Science and Technology.* Copyright © 1965, Mc-Graw-Hill Book Company. Used by permission.

EXHIBIT 7

- Definition of lines.
- Definition of conics.
- Changing scale.
- Rotating about designated axis.
- Translation.
- Free-hand sketching.
- Alphanumeric display.
- Deletion.[4]

Work is being continued by a 20-man team under the direction of S. H. Chasen.

Other companies have more recently become engaged in active development efforts. These efforts typically consist of prototype hardware configurations for R&D purposes.

APPLICATIONS DESCRIBED

Passive computer graphics, we have seen, is particularly appropriate to the solution specification phase of the design process. While it has contributed in many ways to the conceptualization and analysis phases by assisting designers to "see" the problem, the long cycle required to prepare off-line passive graphic materials has inhibited its wider use for this purpose. *Active* computer graphics, on the other hand, permits the designer to interact with the computer in real time.

Nevertheless, some of the first developmental applications for active graphics have been for drafting purposes. This is a result of the software problems associated with dealing with objects rather than drawings that we mentioned earlier. Drafting is the simplest task facing an active graphics system.

In the mechanics of drawing, the computer graphics system can generate lines, circles, arcs, and even free-hand drawing on the face of the scope under operator control. Parts of drawings can be deleted. Drawings, or parts of them, can be magnified or reduced in size. The image can be rotated. Scale can be specified. Distances between points can be automatically calculated and displayed. Repetitive tasks, such as the drawing of all teeth on a gear can be done easily by using a duplicating function. The same techniques of duplication can be applied to the design of an apartment house where many of the layouts are identical. Where there are many uses of the same item in drawings—bolts, rivets, lock-nut as-

[4] Chasen, S. H., "Man-Computer Graphics," *Lockheed-Georgia Quarterly,* Summer 1965, p. 7.

semblies—the computer can be directed to remember the configuration and can be instructed to call that part from memory. Some typical capabilities are shown in Exhibit 8.

With an object described geometrically, it is possible to perform some kinds of analysis. Objects can be subjected to an external force and a stress analysis performed. In his SKETCHPAD demonstration, Ivan Sutherland produced the drawing of a truss bridge on the console. (See Exhibit 9.) The deflection of members as loads were placed on the structure was shown graphically and numerically.

Dr. Frank Skinner's Graphic Methodology Group at IBM's Kingston System Development Laboratory has developed a ten-part demonstration sequence for use with potential computer graphics customers. The design application in the series is an electronic circuit analysis program. This analysis program is for a simple RIC (resistor, inductance, capacitor) network, but the power of computer graphics is evident from the results the program produces. The designer draws his circuit and specifies the values of the components and the shape and value of the input waveform. With this information, the system computes for one or two seconds and then draws the output waveform. If the designer wants to change the value of the components in the circuit, he makes the change right on the screen. As he does so, the computer automatically changes the output waveform. The designer is also free to change the input waveform. The program as designed by IBM gives the man the choice of specifying a square wave or sine wave or of drawing the waveform free-hand. Changes in output are again automatically computed and displayed.

This is, admittedly, a simple circuit on which to perform an analysis. However, it does demonstrate quite well the very valuable dimension added by the graphics system. The designer had previously been able to get the same data from a computer. But it came out of the computer much later as numbers on a sheet of paper. Surely the designer could, and frequently did, plot those numbers on graph paper to see what waveform he actually got.

In the summer of 1965, two IBM systems engineers mated graphics input-output to an existing analysis program, ECAP (Electronic Circuit Analysis Program). ECAP allows alternating current, direct current, and transient analyses of circuits the size of 50 nodes and 200 branches. The present graphic version of ECAP does not have all the analysis power that the original ECAP has. For example, graphics ECAP will not perform on an alternating current worst-case analysis. In addition, as it is now configured, the graphic version will only accommodate 30 nodes and 40 branches

GRAPHIC SYSTEMS CAPABILITIES

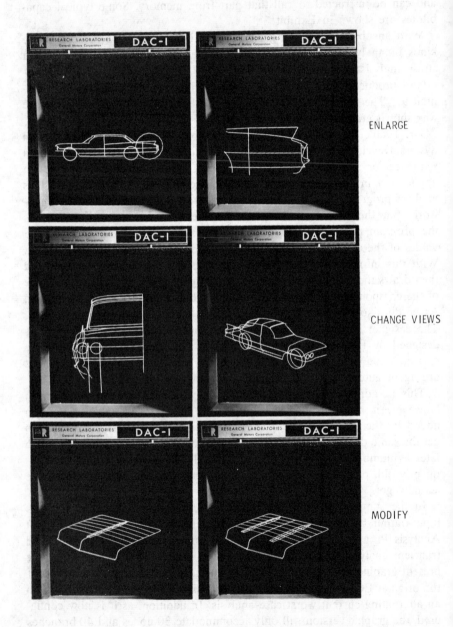

Source: General Motors Corporation. Used by permission.

EXHIBIT 8

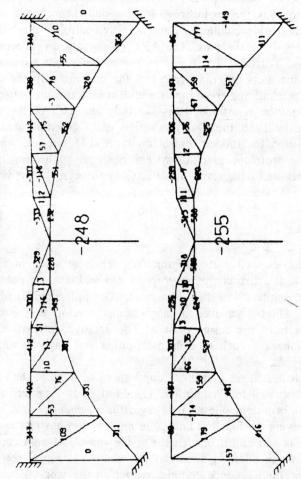

SKETCHPAD TRUSS BRIDGE

(Numbers designate state of stress or deflection in bridge members)
Source: *McGraw-Hill Yearbook of Science and Technology*. Copyright © 1965, Mc-Graw-Hill Book Company. Used by permission.

EXHIBIT 9

rather than the 50 and 200. To have made the complete conversion would have required two or three times the programming effort that was expended. Exhibit 10 shows a designer using ECAP. As it was, some three man-months of programming were involved for the conversion. This program is presently being used on a trial basis for circuit design work within IBM.

At Lockheed-Georgia, the computer graphics system has been applied initially to numerical control parts programming. Formerly, the parts programmer had to copy the engineering drawing and then encode instructions defining the path the cutter of a numerically controlled machine tool should follow to shape the part. The APT (Automatically Programmed Tools) language, a stylized list of geometric commands, was used for this purpose. Now the parts programmer copies the drawing onto the display using the light pen and numerical inputs and then indicates the cutter path. This entire operation is estimated to take only one-sixth of the former time. In February 1966 the first production part, a complicated four-spoked pulley used for rudder control on the C-141 aircraft, was produced using the prototype graphics system. Such an application heralds the marriage between design and manufacturing through the active computer graphics interface.

THE POTENTIAL

Drafting, analysis, and parts programming represent some of the applications to which active computer graphics can and is being put today. These uses are significant in their own right. The full potential of computer graphics will be achieved as applications develop in the earlier, unstructured parts of the design process. The iterative, interactive, real-time man-machine approach to conceptualization and analysis will yield the greatest payoffs.

It is quite possible to see immediate applications to some of the analysis programs we discussed in Chapter III. The Ford Body Engineering program for design of automobile window regulator mechanisms is a case in point. By observing the four-bar linkage in motion, and having the ability to relocate pivots and adjust bar lengths at the console, a man could design a mechanism in minutes. Similarly, the windshield wiper mechanism design program could produce graphics output on the scope as easily as it produces numbers on the printer.

The cockpit vision studies at Boeing are amenable to active graphics output. Rather than using the SC 4020 and producing off-line pictures,

ELECTRONIC CIRCUIT DESIGN ON IBM 2250

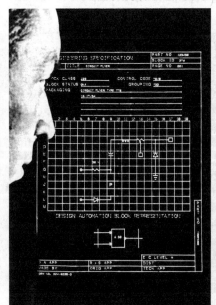
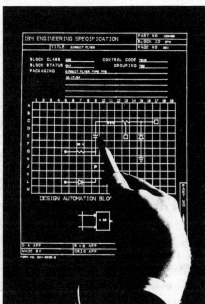
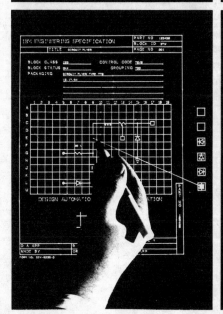
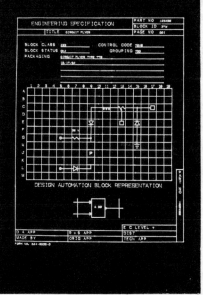

(Designer views circuit on display console, deletes a capacitor, adds a diode for revised circuit)

Source: IBM *Computing Report*, December 1965. Used by permission.

EXHIBIT 10

the designer will be able to sit at the scope and see the effects of his design on such factors as pilot vision.

The day will come when the designer will have the power of a complete computer-aided design system at his disposal, such as we described in our imaginary Helverson Manufacturing Company in Chapter I. Upon seating himself at the console, the system would make available to him his latest version, a broad array of analytical routines, and all the applicable design standards. In an interactive mode he would perfect his design. The system would check for interferences and overall design performance. When he was completely satisfied, the system would proceed to generate the full range of manufacturing specifications, including drawings (where necessary), parts lists, and numerical control tapes.

Most of the pieces of such a system exist today, albeit some are in embryonic form. A fully developed computer graphics system requires advances in the technology of time-sharing, data organization and management, surface definition methods, and graphics programming. Such systems require the largest computer facilities available. Larger, faster, and cheaper memories will assist the development process, as well as improvements in display resolution, stability, and size. The problems are being addressed and will be overcome. In the meantime, present technology permits wider use of active computer graphics systems than has been accomplished in industry today.

In the remainder of this report we will be concerned with the managerial issues of active computer graphics systems. We have laid the groundwork for such considerations in our discussions of the technology.

CHAPTER VI

WHO CAN BEST USE COMPUTER GRAPHICS? •

W E HAVE DEVOTED a good portion of preceding chapters to describing the benefits and savings that many people foresee as the result of full utilization of computer graphics systems in design. Perhaps the most difficult task, however, is determining the relevance of these considerations to a particular company. Sure the benefits sound good, but for whom do they hold the greatest promise? What industry and company characteristics can serve as guidelines for judging the importance of computer graphics?

On considering this issue, we immediately encounter a problem. The industry and company characteristics which suggest potential payoffs from a computer graphics (CG) system are heavily dependent on the state of the art, and computer graphics is undergoing a rapid evolution. Most of the technical obstacles currently encountered by computer graphics are also obstacles for computer technology in general. As a result, they are receiving a high level of continuous attention, and advances are being made regularly. It appears appropriate, therefore, to examine those characteristics which suggest that CG, in its *present* state of development, merits serious consideration, and then to suggest what changes we can foresee as CG systems develop further.

APPROPRIATE INDUSTRY CHARACTERISTICS

The industries for which CG systems are most appropriate are, first of all, those whose *products are technically complex*. The process by which the final design is determined requires the extensive application of the engineering disciplines. Quantitative methods of analysis predominate. Of course, these characteristics suggest only that the computer might be usefully applied; the appropriateness of computer graphics is not self-evident. It is important, therefore, that the primary medium in which the designer works and in which the design is recorded and documented be graphical. This would include the full range of engineering drawings and schematics.

Second, CG is most appropriate in industries where the *product is composed of multiple systems.* This typically means that a number of engineering disciplines are involved. A ship is a good example. The hull configuration must be, at least partially, the result of hydrodynamic considerations. The propulsion system may involve diesel, steam, or even nuclear engineering. The weapons system, electrical system, plumbing system, communication system—all require their own special design skills. As a result, the design organization is compartmentalized. The problems of coordination, communication, and control become difficult. The potential for the CG system to assist in the detection of interferences, in the communicating of changes, and in the maintaining of a record of the latest design suggests that such characteristics are important.

Third, CG is well suited to industries where there are *large engineering staffs.* One automobile manufacturer has a thousand designers and draftsmen in the stamping division alone. Commander Craig of the Ship Systems Command estimates that about 222,000 man-days are involved in designing an average-sized noncombatant ship at the present time. The well-known witticism that aerospace companies measure their engineering staffs by the acre suggests the magnitude of the problem. The fact that such staffs bring with them very costly facilities and high indirect staff costs, as well as a high engineering content in the cost of the final product, would indicate fertile grounds for a device which promises the increase in designer productivity that CG does. This becomes especially true in the face of increasing shortages of skilled engineers.

A fourth important characteristic is that *high performance be required of the product.* Such a requirement makes extensive analysis necessary, and this is an area where CG helps. High standards of performance are characteristic, for example, of the aerospace and automobile industries. The aerospace industry is intimately associated with national goals and the exploration of new frontiers of technology. Failures are costly in terms of national prestige as well as in company reputation. A promising aid such as computer graphics is quickly seized upon. The automobile industry is also faced with a high cost of failure; and failure can occur at performance levels very nearly perfect. A reputation for quality products is easily endangered.

Fifth, the *pertinent technologies should be undergoing a high rate of change.* New production methods, new materials, new design concepts, all suggest the importance of maintaining flexibility for a longer period in the design process. When the consequences of changing a design become so undesirable that the design is effectively frozen, then the benefits of new technology are lost until the next design is undertaken. CG lowers the cost of changes by providing immediate access to the latest design and the mechanism for making an immediate change. In this manner, flexibility can be maintained through later stages in the design process.

A high rate of change in the design can also be the result of deliberate action, as well as of new technology. This is the case in the automobile industry, where prior designs are purposely obsoleted to create new markets.

Sixth, the industries where computer graphics is receiving the most active attention are further characterized by a *small number of highly competitive companies.* Under these circumstances new competitive weapons are quickly seized. It becomes important to be in on the development of new techniques so that the benefits can be quickly obtained. Waiting for others to carry out the development with the intention of capitalizing on their results is a risky strategy. An in-house competence takes time to develop. It becomes difficult to judge whether the motive is the seeking of competitive advantage or the avoiding of a competitive disadvantage.

In defense industries it is important to maintain *a posture of competence,* a seventh important characteristic. One criterion for the awarding of defense contracts is whether the company under consideration is capable of bringing to bear all the latest technology. The importance attached to computer graphics by defense agencies can be seen in the funds being expended to support research efforts such as the Computer-Aided Design project at M.I.T.

APPROPRIATE COMPANY CHARACTERISTICS

All of the companies active in computer graphics are in the top 50 of *Fortune's* 500: they are *large.* The present high cost of development is directly responsible for this fact. Indeed, the earliest entries have all had sales in excess of $1 billion. Further, they have been *experiencing very successful (profitable) operation,* thus making funds available for large, long-term investments. Their competitors who are not currently enjoying such successes are not yet becoming so active.

The companies have *extensive experience in research and development* which provides the know-how for managing large, long-term development projects. In addition, they have accumulated *extensive computer expertise*. One aerospace company is currently operating 138 digital computers of various types and sizes within the corporation. Another is operating five large-scale computers of the IBM 7094 class in one division alone. This high level of sophistication has permitted quick recognition of the long-term significance of computer graphics systems. It also makes the development task seem more manageable, since there is talent on which to draw for systems specification and systems design.

These companies have also all been *exposed to the technology of numerically controlled machine tools*. They are quick to comprehend the benefits of interfacing design and manufacturing through computer graphics parts programming. They have all *used passive graphics techniques*, and this has enhanced their ability to foresee the benefits of active graphics techniques.

Their long and extensive use of computers has resulted in *close relationships with computer manufacturers*. This relationship has provided the opportunity to draw on resources outside their own organizations. We have already noted that the General Motors DAC-I equipment was specially designed by IBM to GM's specifications. Others are drawing on computer manufacturers for programming assistance.

Perhaps the most important characteristic these companies have in common is *a management that is receptive to change and innovation*. The larger CG projects have had to present substantial justification for their expenditures, but the managements concerned have listened with interest. In some cases the management attitude has rapidly become one of quite active and enthusiastic support.

A GLIMPSE AT THE FUTURE

The infant state of the art in computer graphics has meant that some pretty stringent conditions had to be met before a serious project for the development of a computer graphics capability could be undertaken. In industries where there is:

- Technically complex, multiple-system products.
- Large engineering staffs.

- High product performance standards.
- High rate of change in pertinent technologies, or high rate of change in design.
- Small number of highly competitive companies.
- Importance of maintaining a posture of competence.

For companies which have:

- Large size and successful (profitable) operation.
- Extensive experience in R&D.
- Extensive computer experience.
- Experience with numerical control and passive graphics.
- Close relationships with computer manufacturers.
- Management receptive to innovation.

We can expect that, as the technology evolves, the requirements will become less stringent. A number of companies not presently active have already established that CG will be an important tool for them. The only remaining consideration is one of timing. As the technical hurdles are lowered, size and expertise will become less important. The magnitude of the required investment will be reduced as appropriate software becomes generally available. The big mistakes will have been made and the projected benefits will be more certain.

The requirements will always exist that the product be highly engineered and that the principal design medium be graphical. If one sets rather restricted goals for the CG system, however, then some small companies may well be able to justify a system in the near future. If the principal uses were to be for drawing and simple analysis and if the analyses to be accomplished were well known and already performed on computers, then the only requirements would be for a drawing package and the modification of the analysis programs to accept graphical input-output. Architectural firms, electronics firms, and civil engineering firms are examples that come to mind. IBM stated that a number of the IBM 2250 graphics consoles were being delivered to smaller firms such as these in 1966.

There is no doubt that computer graphics systems will show up in many kinds and sizes of companies during the next ten years. Their appearance will be governed by the degree of management receptiveness more than any other single factor.

CHAPTER VII

THE ECONOMICS OF THE COMPUTER
GRAPHICS DECISION •

IN THIS CHAPTER we will consider the economic factors underlying the decision to develop a computer graphics facility. The current state of the art and the limited operational experiences of the few experimental users restrict the amount of economic information obtainable from actual case situations. Nevertheless, we feel that even this limited information allows us to draw some broad conclusions regarding the magnitude and the type of costs and benefits which pertain to an operating system. From these we will develop a framework within which a prospective user can usefully relate the appropriate economic factors to his particular investment decision.

A basic assumption in this chapter is that the user is planning to develop an *operating* computer graphics facility, as distinct from a system which is simply designed to allow his engineering and research laboratories to experiment with the possibilities of computer graphics. In this latter situation, the company is not necessarily expecting any tangible savings to be produced by the facility, and for this reason the investment can be classified simply as a research expenditure. In the development of an operating facility, however, there must be serious consideration of the main economic factors involved—the streams of cash inflows and outflows generated by a computer graphics decision must be fully taken into account. This requires a forecast of the costs, savings, and value of benefits engendered during the period of actual system development and operation. The economic decision can be viewed as a special type of capital investment decision, involving more intangible or unquantifiable benefits than is normally the case.

It is with this point of view in mind that we plan to discuss the investment decision, first by delineating the costs or cash outflows that arise, then by describing the benefits or savings that will hopefully result from the system's operation, and finally by linking these costs and savings together to form a meaningful analysis both at the macro or "feasibility study" level and at the micro or the "new application" level.

TYPES OF COSTS (OR OUTFLOWS)

The development of an operating computer graphics system involves a number of costs for software (programming systems), hardware, and overhead. The magnitude of these costs can vary according to the sophistication of the system and the magnitude of the design applications being attempted. It should also be noted that the costs are time-related—that is, that different costs will occur at different points in time (see Exhibit 1) and that in most cases they are uncertain. This uncertainty suggests that a realistic evaluation of costs would be based on a range within which each cost could vary, rather than on any single figure which represents the mean or expected cost. We will attempt to present the possible costs under the headings of software, hardware, and overhead.

SOFTWARE COSTS

The software necessary to operate a computer graphics system has been described in a previous chapter and includes the following: a monitor system; scheduling and interrupt algorithm; list processors and file organizers; language processors or compilers; a library of frequently used subroutines; and user programs which are applicable to the particular job being run. There are indications that once mature CG systems are used in well-developed applications, computer manufacturers will provide a large part of the first four categories of software and include them, to some extent, in the hardware cost. Currently, however, the companies pioneering in CG have to develop their own programming systems to a large degree; and during interviews with some of these companies, it became apparent that substantial expenses were involved in this software development. One large aerospace company stated that development of an as-yet-incomplete two-dimensional drawing package has already cost 12 man-years of programming effort and about $30,000-40,000 of machine time. The effort of Lockheed-Georgia for CG development, which is mainly in software

AN ILLUSTRATION OF THE TIME DIMENSION OF COSTS AND SAVINGS

YEAR	ACTION	COSTS	BENEFITS OR SAVINGS
0	Decision to develop a CG facility	Personnel; space, systems training	Probably nil
1	Systems specification and software specification		
2	Some software development		
3	Installation of computer hardware		
4	Software development Operational training	Personnel, space, hardware rental	a) Quantifiable inflow resulting from improving design capability
5			b) Nonquantifiable or intangible benefits; e.g., better designs, more products, etc.
6			
7			
8			

NOTE: In reality there is a slow transition between the occurrence of inflows and outflows. Thus the clearly defined breaks that the chart suggests are not actually that distinct.

EXHIBIT 1

and applications studies with some hardware modifications, was approximately at a ten-man level in 1964, at a 15-man level in 1965, and will be at more than a 20-man level in 1966.

In the case of General Motors, D. E. Hart and E. L. Jacks stated that they had a library of software in excess of one million computer instructions. Although they did not indicate the cost of developing this software, which is for experimental use in their DAC-I system, we feel that it was probably in the vicinity of $25 million. We emphasize, however, that that is *our* estimate and is *not* based on costs quoted by General Motors.

Emphasis in development efforts such as these has been on the eventual acquisition of a "full" computer graphics capability, aimed at providing operational programs and procedures for use in the design cycle. Other organizations have tended to emphasize the development of computer assistance to design without current emphasis on graphics. These organizations consider that their systems may be readily adjusted to graphics input-output when it becomes more fully operational. At the present time, however, they are using batch operating mode and punched card input. In such situations effort has already been directed towards the development of methods for expressing dimensions, list processing and file organization, subroutines and application-oriented programs, by the use of existing higher-level languages. Our interviews indicated that efforts such as these also incurred substantial costs.

For example, Commander Donald Craig, of the U.S. Naval Ship Systems Command, in discussing the three-year project being done under the direction of Dr. Bernhard Romberg at Arthur D. Little, which will permit major segments of the detailed design of ships' structure to be done with computer assistance, stated that the project will cost $1.8 million. This project may require about 60 man-years of programming and will result in programs totaling about 150,000 FORTRAN instructions. This project is significant for its codification of the ship structural design algorithm and for its methods of handling large amounts of data.

Of course, all these current developments in basic software are fundamentally original efforts. With no precedent or example to follow, these pioneering users are incurring costs greater than those which will be faced by future users when much of the basic software will most likely be provided by the computer manufacturers. It is reasonable to expect the manufacturers to provide the monitor system, the scheduling and interrupt algorithm for the time-shared computer and, to some extent, the language processors and list processors. As mentioned in earlier chapters, IBM has done some work on converting existing card input, batch processing analysis programs into a form suitable for use with graphic input-output.

The computer graphics system itself holds great promise for assisting in software development. The computer programmer has traditionally suffered from the shortcomings of the batch operating mode, just as the designer has. A bootstrap approach, wherein the CG system is used to develop the programming systems, is eminently attractive. The programmer would use the console to develop his program, initially by coding on the alphanumeric keyboard, and ultimately, perhaps, by simply expressing operations in flow chart form on the scope face. Checkout or program testing would proceed while he monitored the progress by visual means. Such a development requires significant advances in language processors. The problems, however, are under attack, notably by Douglas T. Ross at M.I.T. In the interim, programming using more conventional terminals in a time-sharing mode bears promise. As such programming techniques as these become more generally available, a reduction in the man-hours required for programming and, therefore, in the programming costs involved can be expected. This would help to slow the historical trend toward a higher ratio of programming to hardware costs as the more advanced computer applications are brought into operation.

In summary, then, we feel that software costs to the future user will be significant, but of lower magnitude than those incurred by the pioneering companies.

THE COST OF HARDWARE

Other than software development costs, the most significant cost will be the amortization or rental of the equipment. This equipment will consist of a time-shared computer (or one operated in a multiprogramming mode) with the usual ancillary devices, a large primary memory, substantial direct-access storage, a number of graphic consoles, and some means of graphic, hard-copy input-output. The size of the computer will be largely determined by the number of graphic consoles to be used, the volume of data to be handled, and by whether the company plans to use one central system for both CG and other computer applications.

Many of the users we interviewed were using second-generation computers such as an IBM 7094 or Univac 418, linked to a graphic console such as the DEC 340. These installations are largely experimental and are operated on the basis of one graphic console per central processing unit.

Since most of these users were in the process of changing over to third-generation computers such as the IBM 360 series, we felt it would be more realistic to develop some representative hardware costs based on these more recent types of equipment. Using information obtained from manufacturers, we have developed two representative medium-sized facilities. We stress that these illustrations were developed by the authors and, as such, do not represent either equivalent systems or manufacturer's official system configurations or pricing policies. In addition, no allowance has been made for any differences in software packages that may or may not be reflected in the rental costs. The prices and configurations should be considered as indicative only, as it would obviously be impossible to delineate a hardware package suitable for all applications in a field as complex as computer graphics. We are not prepared to claim that these configurations provide sufficient processing or data-handling capacity to support the indicated number of consoles in all types of applications. Exhibits 2 and 3 illustrate respectively an IBM system 360/40 and a Control Data Corporation Digigraphic System 270. In both cases provision has been made for card readers, printers, and other peripheral equipment.

Although we have emphasized the limitations of our configurations, we feel that the costs do represent a range that will give the reader some feel for the magnitude of the costs involved in such systems. Considering one-shift operation only, the exhibits show that our IBM configuration with four graphic consoles, random-access storage, and an image processor would rent for approximately $33,000 per month. The Digigraphic system with three consoles and a digital plotter is in the range of $20,000-22,000 per month.

These figures are typical of the time-related hardware costs or cash outflows relevant to a capital investment decision. Both the magnitude and the timing of such costs are important.

In this treatment of hardware costs we have ignored the complicating factor of additional hardware that would be required to obtain reliability. It may seem strange to raise this issue in view of the high reliability currently achieved by computers. Operation of computers free of hardware-caused errors or equipment breakdowns typically accounts for 96 to 99 percent of total operating time. Under batch mode operating conditions, the occurrence of detectable machine errors or breakdowns is not a significant problem when in the order of one to four percent. The worst that can happen is that the job then running would have to be re-started. A breakdown affects only the currently running job, and all the necessary

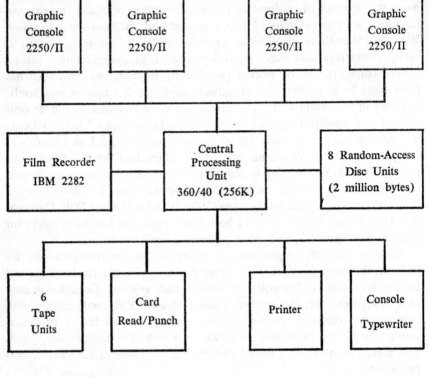

POSSIBLE IBM 360/40 CONFIGURATION AND TYPICAL RENTAL COSTS*

EQUIPMENT	RENTAL/MONTH
Central processor with printer, console, typewriter, card read/punch, and tape units	$17,000
Random-access storage facility	5,500
Total Main Unit	22,500
Four graphic consoles with control unit	5,000
Film recorder	5,500
Total Graphic Units	10,500
TOTAL System	$33,000

NOTE:

1) Details of special features, control units, etc., are omitted for clarity.
2) Rental costs have been rounded.
3) Exhibits 2 and 3 are *not* equivalent.

*These costs were developed by the authors who are solely responsible for this analysis.

EXHIBIT 2

POSSIBLE CDC DIGIGRAPHIC 270 CONFIGURATION AND TYPICAL RENTAL COSTS*

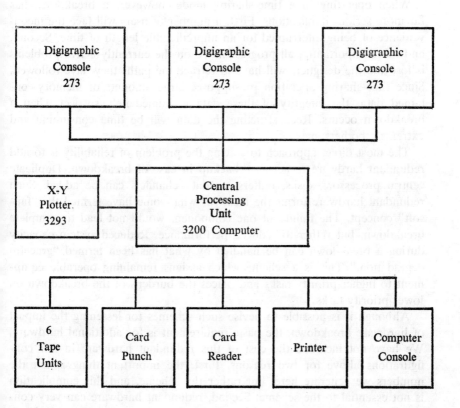

EQUIPMENT	RENTAL/MONTH
Central processor with printer, console, card reader, card punch, tape units, and X-Y plotter	$14,100
Three graphic consoles with control units	5,900
TOTAL System	$20,000

NOTE:
1) Details of special features, control units, etc., are omitted for clarity.
2) Rental costs have been rounded.
3) Exhibits 2 and 3 are *not* equivalent.

*These costs were developed by the authors who are solely responsible for this analysis.

EXHIBIT 3

specifications and data required for a rerun of that job exist external to the computer, usually in the form of punched cards and magnetic tapes.

When operating in a time-sharing mode, however, a breakdown has far more serious implications. First, a number of users will face the inconvenience of being interrupted for an unpredictable length of time. Second, and more importantly, all progress made on the currently active problems is lost and the designers will have to retrace the paths they have followed. Since time-sharing operation presupposes large amounts of memory-contained data, the integrity of these data is immediately suspect when a breakdown occurs. Reconstructing the data will be time consuming and extremely bothersome.

The most direct approach to solving the problem of reliability is to add redundant hardware to act as a backup in case of breakdown. Duplicate central processors, disks, buffers, or data channels can be added. Such redundant hardware forms the basis for what some have termed the "fail-soft" concept. The failure of one component would not lead to complete breakdown, but rather to reduced performance. Reduced system capacity during a breakdown can be handled by what has been termed "graceful degradation." This is a scheme which assigns remaining operable equipment to higher-priority tasks and places the burdens of the breakdown on lower-priority tasks.

Although it is possible to devise such schemes for lessening the impact of hardware breakdown, the basic requirement is for additional hardware. We have not included the cost of this redundant hardware in our configurations above for two reasons. First, the important thing is not the numbers we generate here, but rather the scheme, and this complication is not essential to the scheme. Second, redundant hardware can very conveniently be viewed as a decision ancillary to the main system decision. This is so because the cost and the benefit associated with this hardware are neatly separable from other costs and benefits. Incremental hardware would be rented to achieve a higher degree of reliability. This decision stands alone. Further, redundant equipment may well be usable for batch mode operations which would substantially support the incremental cost.

OVERHEAD COSTS

Operating personnel, space costs, power, indirect personnel, and other normal computer costs will be incurred in an operational CG system. We do not see any reason for these to be materially different from those of any other computer installation, although the original set-up costs may be somewhat greater because of the special requirements of computer graphics.

THE BENEFITS OF COMPUTER GRAPHICS

We now turn to the other type of cash flow, namely the benefits of computer graphics, from which will come the savings or cash inflows during the period of the system's operation.

The benefits or savings accruing from any capital investment decision can be divided into two categories: (1) tangible or quantifiable benefits and (2) intangible or unquantifiable benefits. This distinction assumes increased importance in applications such as computer graphics where many of the hoped-for savings cannot be readily expressed as discernible cash inflows at a specific point in time. This does not mean that these benefits will not give rise to economic advantages for the company, but rather that such savings cannot at the present time be realistically stated in dollar terms. Because of this difficulty, it is all too easy to propose some rather dubious benefits and have them accepted under the guise of their being "intangible." It is our opinion that if benefits cannot be related to economic savings, even though indirectly or in the long term, then such benefits should not influence the decision of whether to develop a computer graphics facility. In other words, for that particular company, such benefits are irrelevant to the capital investment decision.

The factors which determine whether a benefit is tangible or intangible are so closely related to the specific company or industry which is weighing the pros and cons of computer graphics that we do not propose to attempt any such distinction in our discussion of "benefits." Rather, we simply plan to group the benefits of CG as we see them under the following headings: time-associated cost reduction; direct design-time cost reduction; design improvement; materials cost reduction; and competitive advantages. These groupings are not absolutely watertight but do serve to provide a useful framework for the discussion which follows.

TIME-ASSOCIATED COST REDUCTIONS

Perhaps the major saving promised by computer graphics is the overall reduction in the time required from the point when a new product idea is conceived to the point when the product actually reaches the market. This decrease in lead time will bring in its wake many associated and subsidiary benefits, but here we are basically concerned with the increase in overall efficiency which should result from the declining occurrence of those annoying delays which currently characterize the design process. This momentum—the ability to keep the product design rolling once it is under way—should reduce project errors and increase enthusiasm and efficiency among design personnel.

However, other, more tangible benefits exist. The use of computer graphics will allow each designer to accomplish more in less time and, in addition, will allow management, by comparison of the number of hours a designer spends at the console with the quality of the design work he creates, to have more control over the engineer's use of time. An instance of the results of increased engineering productivity is the often predicted reduction in automobile design time from 24 months to six months, through the application of a full-scale computer graphics system. Although this magnitude of reduction is optimistic in the near term, it is indicative of what the future could bring. This theory of lead-time reduction is further supported by Dr. Bernhard Romberg of Arthur D. Little. He has estimated that the new partially automated design system for the Navy will cut detail design time for ship structure from eight months to two to four weeks.

The overall reduction in lead time will provide the ability for the company to react more quickly to changes in the market, thus increasing the potential for being first out with a new design and reducing the risk of producing a product which no longer fits the need. This type of quick reaction will be particularly beneficial in the pursuance of national goals arising under emergency conditions, whether in time of war or peace.

The design group of every company has certain costs which are largely fixed or time-associated. The cost of maintaining physical facilities is one example. By increasing the productivity of individual designers such costs can be reduced since a smaller staff would be required. By increasing the flow of products, while reducing or maintaining such fixed costs, the number of products over which to spread these costs increases. In this manner, the design cost per product can be reduced. This leads us to the next category of benefits.

DIRECT DESIGN-TIME COST REDUCTION

As we have already noted, it should be possible for engineers to perform the same design in fewer man-hours than is possible without the use of CG. If this reduction in time required to perform functions such as drafting is sufficient to offset the cost of using the equipment needed to perform drafting, then the cost of the design will be reduced.

Experience with purely passive graphics drafting machines has indicated that, to a large extent, the dollar savings are usually marginal. O. D. Smith of North American Aviation has stated that costs saved by its AUTO-DRAFT system are marginal when compared to what a draftsman could do manually, except in specialized situations when advantage can be taken of efficient techniques. The AUTODRAFT system utilizes card input to a computer operated in the batch processing mode, and the output is in the form of drawings traced by a variety of passive graphics equipment.

In the case of CG, we do not anticipate such marginal returns. With the design information so readily convertible into digitized form within the computer by the use of the light pen, the man-machine interface will be considerably faster. This digitized form of design information can be stored in the computer files and be available for almost instant recall when and wherever required. Of course, the computer can also be used to drive numerically controlled machine tools or a digital plotter, or to produce hard copy by photographic means. Therefore, many of the limitations of the batch processing of design information are overcome.

It is worthwhile to consider some of these benefits in more detail. The man-machine interface or input to the computer is key to the efficiency with which the designer can handle his task. It is no longer necessary for the designer to worry about drawing straight lines or accurate circles—the machine will automatically allow for any small errors and produce perfectly straight lines and circular circles if desired. In addition, the designer can impose constraints upon his work. For instance, the computer can be made to ensure that particular lines are at right angles. Repetitive tasks can be handled by the machine: one small detail such as a gear tooth can be repeated many times. Many of the "mechanical" drafting functions that previously delayed the designer will now be performed by the machine.

The real-time operation of the graphics console means the designer no longer has to wait hours for results—hours he must spend in another activity. He doesn't need to recall and re-think his original conceptualization, rather, his thought process can be continuous. Further, his communication with the computer can be in the most natural language to him: graphics. He isn't required to spend time recasting his problems into an artificial language.

We have mentioned that the drawings can be stored in digitized form within the computer. This has several advantages helpful in providing savings. One of these was suggested by one large aerospace company, which stated that about 20 percent of the activity in relation to any drawing is the initial preparation, while 80 percent is change and correction. When this is compared to the number of drawings required by large aircraft of the 1950's—20 to 25,000—or by the even more complex and larger aircraft of today—100 to 200,000—it is clear that an increase in drawing efficiency will generate substantial savings and, further, that the need for these savings is growing. By having the drawing filed in the computer, the designer no longer has to fear making changes. It becomes a simple matter to update the master computer file from the console and in effect update all the copies. When a person uses a remote console to view a particular drawing, he is always looking at the most recent copy and the likelihood of mistakes resulting from the use of outdated information, is greatly reduced.

The retention of the design in a digitized form allows the data to be readily manipulated in a variety of ways. Perhaps one of the more dramatic is the ability to evaluate the design's performance prior to building a prototype. The "performance evaluation" stage of designing evolved in the following way. Initially, the major form of evaluation was by actual use. Then the test track or its equivalent provided a means of accelerating the evaluation. This latter method was supplemented by the testing of prototypes under simulated conditions in the laboratory. It now seems highly probable that there will be a reduced reliance on prototypes. Rather, a design will be evaluated in the form of its mathematical model contained in digital form in the computer. Considerable time and materials savings could arise from this unique feature of computer graphics. Each step in this evolution of evaluation methods has led to increased concern for the degree to which the newest method reflects reality. As a result, the older methods continue to be retained as final tests of performance.

During the course of our interviews, a number of companies voiced the expectation that the use of computer graphics or equivalent techniques would yield significant returns because of the reduction in direct design time. Lockheed-Georgia talked of its parts-programming system for numerical control machine tools using computer graphics, which is expected to break even at a reduction in parts-programming time of 3:1. The actually anticipated time savings in parts programming is 6:1 or greater. The company also expects a significant reduction in errors on the N/C tapes produced by this system, and a reduction in span time from the two or three days presently required to produce a satisfactory N/C tape to less than one day.

On the basis of our discussions at General Motors, we concluded that there might be areas in the design process at that company where paybacks in excess of 17:1 could be obtained by the use of the CG system. In the Naval Ship Systems Command, the total planned program ($100 million) in ship design, of which Dr. Romberg's project is a part, is expected to yield a payback of at least 14:1 over the 20-year project. Commander Craig indicated that a number of segments of the project offered full payback within six months of full implementation. The Ford Motor Company has found that about 10 percent of the engineering and design problems run in traditional batch mode in the computer center have yielded savings sufficient to cover the total cost of the computer center five times over. The other 90 percent of the problems have included the performance of operations impossible without a computer, and therefore the economic effect was difficult—and unnecessary—to assess.

These examples are indicative of the direct cost reductions which are apparently feasible through the use of computer graphics in the design cycle. They will serve as useful guideposts when we come to discuss a method of deciding which applications can economically be placed on the CG facility.

DESIGN IMPROVEMENT

The new freedom provided for the designer by the man-machine interface will act as a stimulant to creativity. The rapid interplay made possible between the man and the machine will enable the designer to try more alternatives, to view the results almost instantaneously, and to obtain a "feel" for the phenomenon he is observing. This immediate reinforcement, coupled with easy modification capability, will allow the designer to work and think in a manner unrestricted by the physical limitations associated with present design methods. We feel that this freedom will serve to make the designer more creative and to bring about an improvement in the standard of designs. Many people we talked to felt one of CG's greatest benefits would be this "enrichment of the design environment."

A further design improvement resulting from CG is what is known as "interference reduction." This problem arises when many designers are working on the same product either in different physical locations or on different systems of the same product. In cases like these, it is quite possible for one designer to design a part that "interferes" with some other part of the design. Examples of this might be when holes are not changed in a bulkhead although a change has been made in the electrical system, or when some addition to an engine mounting obstructs the position of a fuel line. These problems become particularly troublesome in large designs such as aircraft or shipbuilding, and, unfortunately, they are often not discovered until tooling or even production are well under way. Computer graphics, through its ability to retain drawings in its memory, reduces the probability of such occurrences. A designer at a console in one part of the plant can readily access and interpret the same up-to-date information available to all, and the likelihood of interference problems is minimized. This allows for an increased reliability in the finished design as it leaves the engineering department.

Apart from providing access to a central computer library of engineering drawings, CG also provides the means by which an engineer or designer can access a central library of engineering information—such as the latest abstracts on technical developments or an index which allows him to find quickly references to articles published in his area of interest. Such an information retrieval system would assist the designer in keeping abreast of the field and encourage him to incorporate the latest technical advances in his designs.

Of course, the sheer ability to design more rapidly will give rise to improved designs. It will now be possible to more readily incorporate into the finished product last-minute modifications that might have previously been rejected because of the inflexibility of the last stages of the design process. This increased ability to modify designs will allow more special orders to be fulfilled, and this has obvious implications for the company's competitive position.

MATERIALS COST REDUCTION

A major benefit, which we shall classify as materials cost reduction, is the designer's new ability to avoid the overengineering of safety margins. Simulation testing on the computer can help reduce unnecessary safety margins while still ensuring the required performance. This ability can provide major materials-cost savings, especially in mass-produced products. One automobile manufacturer stated that millions of dollars had been saved by seemingly minor materials savings. CG offers the opportunity for achieving substantial savings of this sort more often.

Other claims that may be made for a reduction in the cost of materials are really related to reductions made in the number of errors committed during the design process, such as undetected interference problems, in the number of drawing changes that occur after production parts have been purchased and production is under way, and in the accuracy or completeness of manufacturing specifications. The connection between these factors is not immediately obvious; but, as the use of CG ensures improved design, so the late changes and errors caused by the use of outdated or incorrect drawings will be reduced. The reduction of materials losses accruing from this type of improvement will be impossible to quantify accurately, because the cost of avoided errors can never be known. In spite of this, we feel that considerable reductions in production-materials usage will result from the use of CG. Further, this statement makes no allowance for the materials savings that will arise from a reduction in drawing office supplies, through the use of less hard copy, and also because of the need to produce fewer, if any, prototypes during the design phase of the product.

COMPETITIVE ADVANTAGES

Computer graphics as a design tool provides the possibility of improving a company's performance vis-a-vis that of its competitors. The reduction in design cycle time facilitates the preparation of faster, more accurate and more detailed contract proposals. A shorter and less expensive design process will enable companies in such industries as aerospace to become more competitive in their bidding. Lockheed-Georgia stated that the preliminary design for the C-5-A required about $20 million, of which it recovered about $12 million. This highlights the important role that design assumes in some bidding situations.

We have already hinted at the ability of the computer graphics company to adapt itself more quickly to changes in the marketplace. The product can be adapted more rapidly and modified to suit changing tastes. This assumes tremendous importance in highly competitive market situations.

The growing glamor of CG could also produce beneficial side effects for the company with a developed facility. We would predict that in the years ahead, the best engineers will wish to work at companies which make use of such techniques. Although this may not seem to be an important advantage, it assumes increased stature when considered against the growing technical complexity of this age and the increasing shortage of first-class design engineers. Depending on the nature of the product and the type of industry, the ability to attract the best-qualified engineers could become a definite competitive advantage.

In the preceding pages, we have attempted to delineate the major benefits of CG to the potential user. We requested that the reader should consider these as tangible and intangible savings playing a definite role in the computer graphics capital investment decision. We turn now to the specific decision itself and to the manner in which costs and benefits are matched in order that a basis for the economic justification of acquiring a computer graphics facility may be provided.

THE ECONOMIC RELATIONSHIP OF COSTS AND BENEFITS

When considering the economics of a computer graphics facility, it is necessary to clearly distinguish between two separate situations. The first is the feasibility study wherein the company attempts to determine the initial feasibility of acquiring a computer graphics facility. This study aims at determining whether the company will be economically better off with or without a CG capability and, needless to say, should be performed before any definite commitment is made to hardware or software outlays. The second situation assumes that the company already has an operating CG capability, in which case the problem is to decide which particular applications should be put on the equipment and which are better performed by existing methods.

As these are two separate problems, we plan to make a clear distinction between them in this chapter. It should be noted, however, that application studies are to some extent dependent upon facts used in the feasibility study. We will highlight such relationships where they exist.

THE FEASIBILITY STUDY

The feasibility study is largely a capital investment decision. In the initial stages of CG development, it is impossible to determine accurately all the exact costs, savings, and benefits that will result from a decision to develop computer graphics. However, it is known that these inflows and outflows will occur at different points in time and that some will be more certain than others. We assume here that the type and costs of hardware have been determined and that *general* categories of applications have been ascertained and ranked in a time sequence according to their proposed dates of introduction to the equipment.

Having determined these broad areas of application, we must carefully delineate such savings or benefits as will accrue. Where actual cash savings can be determined, they should be calculated and ranked according to when they will be realized. Many of the benefits will be unquantifiable, and these should be explicitly determined and their nature and extent noted in qualitative terms. We should determine three types of flows: first, costs or cash outflows ordered in an appropriate time sequence; second, tangible or quantifiable cash inflows ordered according to when they will occur; and third, an explicit listing of the unquantifiable or intangible benefits that will accrue from the development of a CG facility.

This brings us to the mechanics of a capital investment decision. Among the several ways of making such a decision, the most popular are:

- Ranking alternatives by inspection.
- Ranking by the pay-back period, which is defined as the length of time required for the stream of cash inflows produced by an investment to equal the original cash outlay.
- Ranking alternatives according to the rate of return on investment.
- Using the discounted cash flow or present-value method of ranking investments.

For our present purposes, we will use the last method—that is, the present-value method.[1] This approach has many virtues, but perhaps its main one is that it takes full account of the fact that money has a time value. Inflows or outflows of cash associated with the investment and occurring some time in the future have a different value for the company than inflows or outflows occurring now.

An example may serve to illustrate this principle. The present value of $100 payable in three years can be defined as the amount of money needed to be invested today to give $100 in three years, where the initial sum is subject to compound interest. Assuming that the rate of interest is 5 percent and is compounded annually, we know that $1 invested today under these conditions would, at the end of three years, grow to $1.1576. To find the present value at 5 percent of $100 in three years, we divide $100 by $1.1576, which gives us $86.38. Thus $86.38 invested at 5 percent would be worth $100 at the end of three years. By repeated applications of this method we can convert any series of current or *future* cash flows into an *equivalent* present value. By such a method we make adequate allowance for the timing of future cash proceeds, and in effect we remove the time element from our decision by reducing all cash flows to the same level—that is, their present value. Since tables giving all the necessary conversion factors for various rates of interest and time periods are available, these calculations are not difficult to make.

---

[1] A full discussion of this technique can be found in Bierman, Harold, and Seymour Smidt, *The Capital Budgeting Decision,* The MacMillan Company, New York, 1960.

In order to perform the present-value analysis in our feasibility study, we need the three flows described earlier, as well as a rate of interest with which to discount the cash flows. For the purposes of this discussion we are assuming a requirement that the investment make a return in excess of some predetermined "hurdle" rate. In an actual situation this might be the cost of capital or some other figure that the company feels is appropriate. Having these four factors, it is possible to complete a present-value calculation. A hypothetical example is presented in Exhibit 4.

When the calculation is performed, it is possible to end up with a present value that is either positive, zero, or negative. If the present value is either positive or zero, then the tangible cash inflows will outweigh the costs involved at the hurdle rate used. Under these criteria, the system is economically justified, and any intangible benefits that also accrue will only serve to strengthen the decision. On the other hand, if the present value turns out to be negative, then the hurdle rate is not met. It now becomes a qualitative decision in which management must weigh the intangible benefits, as were explicitly listed, against the present-value "cost" which the calculation revealed. (Exhibit 4 shows such a negative present value.) If management feels the intangibles are worth this cost, then the investment should proceed; but if the cost is too high for these unquantifiable benefits, then the investment should be postponed. The balancing off of intangible benefits in this way allows management to make a more realistic appraisal of the economic justification for a computer graphics facility.

We have mentioned previously that many of the cash flows are uncertain and that it is advisable to reflect this uncertainty by putting a range on the figures involved. It is then possible to calculate the present value under both the pessimistic and optimistic alternatives. A range of present values is determined which reflects the uncertainty of the cash flows. Such a technique is a more realistic approximation to the economic factors underlying the investment decision.[2]

THE ECONOMIC DESIRABILITY OF PARTICULAR CG APPLICATIONS

In developing the present-value analysis described above, the savings or benefits to be derived from the facility could have been determined by

[2] For a more sophisticated consideration of this uncertainty problem, the interested reader is referred to Hertz, David B., "Risk Analysis in Capital Investment," *Harvard Business Review,* January-February 1964.

HYPOTHETICAL PRESENT-VALUE ANALYSIS
(All figures in thousands of dollars)

Year**	(1) Cash Outflows Hardware costs Software costs Other costs	(2) Cash Inflows Tangible saving arising from CG operation	(3) Difference	(4) Discount* Factor	(3x4) Cash Flow Discounted
1	− 600	+ 100	− 500	.909	− 450
2	− 650	+ 250	− 400	.826	− 340
3	− 650	+ 450	− 200	.751	− 150
4	− 700	+ 600	− 100	.683	− 68
5	− 700	+ 1000	+ 300	.621	+ 186
6	− 1000	+ 1500	+ 500	.564	+ 280
7	− 1000	+ 1700	+ 700	.513	+ 360
					− 182

Thus, at 10% rate, the present value
of the investment over 7 years is $182,000

* Assumes 10% hurdle rate. Factors obtained from present-value table.

** The number of years included is an estimate of the length of time this
equipment will be in operation before investment changes are made.

EXHIBIT 4

considering the timing of the development of "broad categories of applications." An example of the development of such categories might be the operational introduction of a two-dimensional drawing package. In assessing the desirability of a general package, it is necessary to determine the *"ultimate* utilization rate" of the central processing unit by the graphic consoles.

The "ultimate utilization rate" may be defined as the percentage of central processing unit time that will be required by any *one* graphic console when that console is operating under the fully operational package. If for every hour that a console is used for two-dimensional drawing the central processing unit provides an average of nine minutes of time to perform computations and manipulate data, the utilization rate would be 15 percent. Clearly, the ultimate utilization rate will vary widely, since the requirements for computing and data handling will vary according to the nature of the application package. A two-dimensional drawing package will, in general, not place as heavy a demand on the central processing unit as a simulation to analyze performance.

The ultimate utilization rate is useful when planning capacity needs. The rates, when coupled with the *number* of consoles to be used, will indicate the demands that will be placed on the central processor. If the utilization rate for a two-dimensional drawing package were 15 percent, then the system could only service six graphics consoles using that package at any one time (6 x 15 percent = 90 percent). The fact that the time would be allocated in very small segments is what permits all six to be serviced "simultaneously." Should the capacity not be sufficient, a faster central processor could be considered, or the use of smaller local computers servicing a limited number of consoles may solve the problem. Since the demand for central processor time will increase as application packages are implemented, it is probable that the hardware configurations would be expanded in stages. Such a plan would, of course, be reflected in the projected cash outflow used in the feasibility study.

In assessing the impact of ultimate utilization rates on capacity, it is necessary to consider any non-CG requirements to be placed on the machine. If the system is to be operated in the multiprogramming mode, we would multiply the utilization rate by the number of consoles to get the central processor time that will be available for batch-processed "background" programs.

The ultimate utilization rate also serves a significant function in assessing the *economic* desirability of a proposed application package. We will proceed now to demonstrate its use for this purpose. This type of problem, as contrasted to the feasibility study, is amenable to a payback method of analysis, because the time dimension is not as significant a factor.

To present a specific example of this technique, we refer back to Exhibit 2 in this chapter, which outlined our estimate of the monthly rental cost of an IBM 360/40 system with four graphic consoles. The rental cost of the main frame is nearly $130 an hour assuming one shift, 176-hour operation, while *each* console rents for approximately $15 per hour under similar assumptions. Since these are approximate figures for a hypothetical system, it is appropriate to consider that the main unit rental might be in the range of $110 to $160 per hour and the console in the $10 to $20 per hour range. Assuming an ultimate or final utilization of the *central processor* of 15 percent, and allocating the full cost of the central processor for this period of time, the rental cost per hour of console use would range from $25 to $40. If the final utilization rate is estimated to be 25 percent, the cost per console per hour would be somewhat higher at about $35 to $60 per hour, but, of course, more work would be accomplished. These utilization rates assume a time-shared computer which has users other than computer graphics for the remainder of the time. It is important to note that although in a time-shared system the operator may sit at the graphic console for the best part of the full hour, the speed of the central processor compared with the speed of the operator is so great that the central processor unit (CPU) will be operating for only a fraction of the time that the operator is at the input unit. The percentages we have used above are based on the experience obtained by General Motors through its operation of one console on the DAC-I system.

Another point relates to this use of the ultimate utilization rate of the central processor. This final rate is used because any application must still be justifiable when the full computer graphics facility is in operation, even though this may be five to seven years away. At that point in time, large CG systems, made up of a number of applications packages, may use the full capacity of the central processor. Therefore, other uses of the machine will not be able to help support the equipment costs. If this is to be the case, then even the initial CG applications in the first year must still be justified at a console cost per hour that incorporates a full allocation of central processing unit costs, even though the early CG applications packages may only use a small part of the machine's capacity. By using the *ultimate* utilization rate it is possible to ensure that the applications will still be justifiable in five to seven years' time when the full costs of the equipment must be supported.

An example of a large time-shared console system is illustrated in Exhibit 5. Here an IBM 360/67 configuration is proposed. For purposes of demonstration we have assumed the capacity to service 100 consoles in real-time. By performing calculations similar to those used previously, but assuming an ultimate utilization of 100 percent of the CPU capacity, the cost per console per hour on one shift is $15 to $30. These examples are indicative only; and as they do not include software or other costs, they should be considered as merely illustrative.

Having now determined equipment cost per hour per console, we must consider the savings or benefits that might result from a particular application. In order to reflect the amortization of set-up and software development costs, we assume that the total operating cost of the system is in the range of $50 to $100 per hour per console. If we also assume that a designer's time is worth about $10 per hour, then a saving of 5 or 10 hours of *his* time would be sufficient to have the use of the system break even. If a designer can do a job at the console in one hour which might have taken five to ten hours without it, then the use of the system outlined will be worthwhile. Of course, particular applications may also include savings other than designer's time; but if payoffs in the ratio of 5:1 or 10:1 can be achieved when only the designer's time is considered, then further savings will merely serve to reinforce the value of the application. Earlier in this chapter, we cited several users who are either currently getting, or else expecting, savings in the range from 6:1 to 17:1. These compare favorably with our payback estimates of from 5:1 to 10:1.

The economic desirability of a particular CG application is determined by comparing the cost per console per hour, based on the final or ultimate CPU utilization rate, to the savings that will accrue from the applications. If the savings are greater than the costs, then the application is justified.

If this payback approach is used for particular applications and if the timing of the introductions of the broad categories of application that were developed in the feasibility study are maintained, then the present-value analysis described earlier will have presented a true picture of the economic merits of a CG facility. There is a relationship and consistency in using the present-value method for the feasibility study and the payback method for particular computer graphics applications.

A LOOK IN SUMMARY

In this chapter we have discussed a method which allows the effective handling of the economic considerations surrounding the computer graph-

TYPICAL RENTAL COST OF 360/67 SYSTEM*

EQUIPMENT	RENTAL/MONTH
Central processing unit (approximately 2 million byte memory)	$110,000
Random-access storage facility (2 billion bytes)	52,500
100 graphic consoles with control units	99,500
3 film recorder/scanners	34,500
TOTAL	$296,500

NOTE:

Details of special features, control units, etc. have been omitted for clarity.

* These costs were developed by the authors who are solely responsible for this analysis.

EXHIBIT 5

ics decision. Software development is, clearly, the major cost that will be encountered. Pioneering users are experiencing large expenditures for their programming systems, but this cost can be expected to decline significantly in the years ahead. We have found hardware costs to be such that, even when coupled with the amortization charges for one-time expenditures, they compare favorably with the kinds of payoffs users are experiencing and projecting.

We have suggested that a present-value analysis is most appropriate for the feasibility study. This permits an effective handling of intangible costs, since they can be compared to the net cost (should there be one) resulting from the analysis. A subjective appraisal can be made by management of their value. A payback analysis appears most useful for decisions concerning specific application packages.

CHAPTER VIII

CONDITIONS FOR SUCCESS •

WHEN CONSIDERING the problem of introducing a new computer application into the company, it is useful to keep in mind three basic factors —namely, the equipment, the state of the art, and the people involved. For the purposes of this discussion, equipment means the type of computer hardware needed to do the job and raises such questions as memory size, number and location of terminals, type of random-access devices, and so forth. The state of the art refers to the match between the application that management has in mind and the body of knowledge and equipment that exists to do the job. Needless to say, one would expect that more start-up and operating problems would be experienced when putting in a pioneering application for which there is little or no precedent than when, say, computerizing the payroll. The final, most difficult, and without a doubt the most important factor is that of people. The people we refer to are the technical personnel, the operating personnel, and management.

It is our opinion that in many feasibility studies too much attention is paid to the hardware problems. All types and sizes of machines are considered and debated at length, no doubt because such problems are much easier to quantify and discuss than are the more qualitative aspects such as people requirements. It is our firm belief that the success of any installation is almost directly proportional to the amount of attention paid to the people problem. This entails direct, hard thinking on the problems of who should manage the system, where it should be placed in the organization, how directly involved the general management should become in the computer's operation, and so on. Lip service to this aspect is simply not good enough to ensure a successful operation.

This chapter will attempt to look at the critical problems which must be considered when installing a computer-aided design system. The three factors—equipment, the state of the art, and people—will not always be explicitly mentioned, but they form a backdrop or framework against which many operating or implementation decisions can be usefully evaluated. The successful consideration of each offers the key to an effectively operating installation.

THE CRITICAL NATURE OF THE IMPLEMENTATION PHASE

In a study by McKinsey and Company entitled "Getting the Most Out of Your Computer," John T. Garrity points to some indicators that suggest reasons why only nine of a group of 27 major U.S. corporations surveyed were obtaining above-average results from their computer installations. Three of the more important indicators mentioned were "the organizational level of the corporate computer executive, the involvement of operating management, and the caliber of the technical staff." There appeared to be a correlation between the companies that had satisfactorily handled these issues and the companies which were obtaining above-average results from their installations. All of these matters are effectively decided during the implementation phase, either by design or default. Once in operation, they are extremely difficult to change. There is reason to believe that similar factors are equally applicable to the development of the CG facility in the organization.

Another useful way of appreciating the critical nature of the CG implementation period is to consider the nature of the task to be performed. Using the experience that has been generated from the use of computers in "normal" business applications, we can observe a range of tasks that have been implemented. Often the simplest and first to be installed is that of payroll accounting. A manual system is usually effectively in operation before the computer is installed—it was simply a matter of almost directly transferring from manual to machine operation. At the other end of the scale, however, is the use of the computer in "operational" systems such as inventory control, production scheduling, and the like. Here the applications are considerably more difficult to implement. The organizational impact on the company is greater as are the risks involved. Offsetting these negative aspects, however, is the fact that the returns and payoffs of a *satisfactorily* implemented "operational" or "logistics" type system are considerably in excess of the benefits gained from merely automating the payroll. If we consider computer-aided design or computer graphics as one step further along the road of complexity and difficulty in implementation, it becomes apparent how important it is to found the operation upon the solid base of a well-conceived policy. Unlike the production or inventory control system, the design process is currently not well structured. Much remains to be done in codifying and, in fact, understanding the actual nature of the design process and its relation to the graphical man-machine interface. The elimination of much unnecessary vagueness in this area will provide the means for the company to obtain a high return on its investment of men, machines, and time. Because the problems of application for each particular company are so immense, they can only be satisfactorily attacked in the long term by a careful implementation in the initial phases. A successful implementation phase is indeed critical for success.

THE ROLE OF A "CHAMPION"

In our many company and government interviews, we were interested in the means by which the various organizations had become seriously interested in computer-aided design systems. We noticed that, in many cases, the driving force had originated from one person who championed the cause from its inception. When Dr. Romberg of Arthur D. Little was questioned on this score, he replied, "There is usually a champion who builds the case for it, and he is not necessarily computer-oriented." Such would appear to be the situation in the United States Navy, where Commander Craig has been largely responsible for introducing the idea of computer-aided design into the Navy's thinking. At Lockheed-Georgia, a dual role of champion has been played by M. D. Prince and S. H. Chasen, who are known in many circles as most ardent advocates of computer design techniques. E. L. Jacks and D. E. Hart at General Motors, have similarly been effective champions.

At the current state of the art, the role of champion seems to be one of the necessary ingredients for the justification and implementation phases of computer graphics. We feel that this is because of the relative lack of knowledge of computer graphics on the part of many managers. The system is expensive, it is new, and it ultimately requires a tremendous upheaval in the engineering *and* other functional areas of the company. The implementation phase is likely to be very long, and initial returns may well be delayed for some years. This rather unique combination of risk and uncertainty requires the services of a farsighted individual who is willing to fairly evaluate the pros and cons of computer graphics, and who will provide the initial impetus to start the ball rolling. Without such a champion, the sheer scope and far-reaching implications of computer-aided design will cause many proposals to founder before they get started. Professor Herzog of the University of Michigan has described this need to "sell management on the idea" as the single greatest barrier to the acceptance of computer-aided design.

Turning now to specific "conditions for success," this area will be reviewed under the following headings: the location of the computer-aided design project in the organization; personnel requirements; technical difficulties; control problems; and finally, management's critical role.

LOCATION IN THE ORGANIZATION

We have noted that computer time-sharing techniques have paved the way for the economic operation of computer-aided design, since time-sharing allows the large central computer to be used for a variety of tasks within the company. It also allows the central computer to be physically located at a point remote from the engineering and R&D departments. Because of this freedom, we will look at computer-aided design as an entity in itself, with access to some centrally located computer. This central computer will be assumed to be either already in use, or else as part of a plan in which it will be used by departments not directly concerned with the application of computer graphics to the design process.

To ascertain the relationship of computer-aided design to the overall organization, it is necessary to digress momentarily to review the three distinct but overlapping phases necessary for the successful development of any computer system: the systems specification phase, the systems design phase, and the programming phase. These phases indicate the stages that any one computer application project must go through before it is an operating reality.

The systems specification phase, in the case of computer-aided design, requires the delineation of the objectives that the new design procedure will hope to accomplish. Aspects of design which will initially be converted—drafting, computation, analytical techniques, and so forth—must be defined; and the types or classes of product or products on which the new system will first be used must be determined—parts to be produced on numerically controlled machine tools, automobile body styling, and so on. Then comes the matter of deciding priority scheduling: what design applications are dependent upon others having been completed, which are the most important to the company and why, and others. The systems specification phase, then, is the formulation of a conceptual framework that integrates the overall implementation of computer-aided design into the company. This phase results in a plan for the stage-by-stage changeover from the present manual design system to the use of the computer. It includes the basic decisions on what information should be provided by the system and under what conditions.

The *systems design phase* is concerned with the factors that are important to the actual development of the selected applications. The volume and activity rates for various kinds of data are anticipated. The nature and frequency of various kinds of input and inquiries are determined; the proper logical sequences required to serve the variety of demands to be placed on the system by users of the application are specified. The purpose of this phase is to design application packages that will implement most efficiently the systems specified in the prior phase, while building toward some sort of ultimate integrated system. A high degree of technical competence in computer hardware and programming techniques is essential to the people engaged in this process. The results of this phase take the form of flow charts and file designs, as well as recommendations on equipment selection.

The final phase of each application package is *the programming phase*. This phase is concerned with the actual software buildup, or program writing, that allows the equipment to fulfill the objectives determined by the systems specification phase and does so in the manner specified in the systems design phase.

Having defined these three phases, it is now possible to ascertain how they tie in with a consideration of the relationship of computer-aided design to the company's organizational structure. Computer-aided design is a complex and highly sophisticated information system. It is specialized, in the sense that its application is to the design process. In the initial stages, the exploratory investigations of computer graphics will be confined to the engineering department and to the research and development laboratories. Additionally, we view its progress as evolutionary, as distinct from revolutionary. We see the impact of the technique slowly spreading from an initial start in a research laboratory, on to the engineering side of the company, and from there out into almost all the functional areas. During this evolutionary period, it is important to keep clearly separated the role and purpose of the three phases—the systems specification phase, the systems design phase, and the programming phase— because as the technique spreads, a separation and distinction between the three phases will become increasingly critical to success.

Consider, then, the case of a company which is planning to go ahead with a computer graphics system. Initially, a special group will be formed to determine the type of information the equipment should process as well as formulate a timetable that can serve as a control device on the systems implementation. This is the systems specification phase. At this stage, it may be desirable to subdivide the group into two units which will consider near- and long-term aspects respectively. This technique has been adopted by Lockheed-Georgia and others to ensure that near-term applications are operating on the computer as soon as possible, thus enhancing an early payback on the initial investment. In any event, as the initial equipment delivery date draws nearer, more time will have to be spent on the systems design phase and the programming aspects. As the use of computer graphics is proved in this rather "research" type of environment, the number of practical applications will grow and its use will begin to spread throughout the engineering and research facilities.

As this spread takes place, the nature of the implementation group will begin to change. The people concerned with the systems specification phase will start to include representatives from other parts of the company. It is interesting to note that Lockheed has an active "Computer-Aided Design/Computer Graphics Users Group" which coordinates related activities throughout the corporation. Functional specialists will be called in to work on the aspects of the system that affect them and their departments. Systems specification takes on a decentralized nature. In contrast to this, the other two phases of system implementation will tend to remain central to R&D, and primarily oriented to the basic hardware and programming aspects of the system.

We view the place of computer-aided design in the organization as being dynamic in character. This is illustrated in the accompanying Exhibit, where two stages in the growth of computer-aided design systems group is maintained by an executive who is no more than *one* level down from the chief executive. The importance of this and of management's participation in the project will be more fully discussed later in this chapter. Also of interest is the shift of the systems specification team to a staff position and its growing ties with the corporate planning group. This latter link is included because of the overall impact we envisage computer-aided design having on the total organization as it reaches out to link sales, production, and finance more closely with design.

THE PLACE OF COMPUTER GRAPHICS IN THE ORGANIZATION

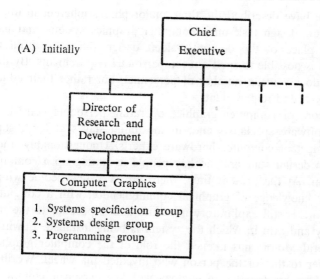

(A) Initially

Chief Executive

Director of Research and Development

Computer Graphics

1. Systems specification group
2. Systems design group
3. Programming group

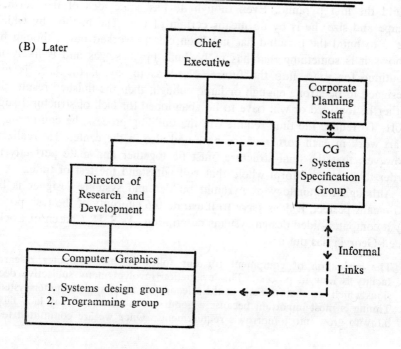

(B) Later

Chief Executive

Corporate Planning Staff

CG Systems Specification Group

Director of Research and Development

Computer Graphics

1. Systems design group
2. Programming group

Informal Links

PERSONNEL REQUIREMENTS

Now that we have described the three major phases inherent in implementing any new design task on a computer graphics system, and have looked at the place of the computer-aided design function within the organization, it is possible to spell out the personnel requirements. By this, of course, we do not mean number of personnel, but rather their educational and background requirements.

The basic core of computer graphics operating personnel consists of systems and software specialists and, in the initial stages at least, some technically competent computer hardware experts. Unquestionably, those on the systems design staff are the key people in setting up a computer graphics system. At the present time, there are very few people with a background or knowledge of graphical communication with a computer. Most of the work is still exploratory in nature and is peculiar to the particular industry and firm in which the system is being installed. Edwin L. Jacks of General Motors has likened the role of the computer graphic's systems designer to that of the person who invented the wheel. We illustrate his task here by drawing an analogy with the person attempting to build the first pyramid. Even though he has some idea of the finished shape and size, he is by no means certain of this. The method by which he is to build the pyramid has not been clearly worked out, although he knows it is something that has to be built up in stages and is likely to continue for years into the future. Needless to say, if the base is not designed to be strong enough or large enough, then the finished result will either be lopsided or will have to be abandoned for lack of structural support. To reduce the time required in the building process, he can perhaps start work in each corner of the base and also in the center. He realizes, however, that the final structure must tie together and mate perfectly in order to form a uniform whole that will withstand the test of time.

Although the analogy of pyramid builder and systems designer is by no means perfect, it does serve to illustrate the enormity of the task posed by a computer-aided design systems description. As S. H. Chasen of Lockheed-Georgia has put it:

> The evaluation of equipment for our follow-on man-computer research facility is now in process. This evaluation involves many subjective decisions which are characteristic of the selection of any major computer system. Timing is most important because a good system for today may lack flexibility to grow into tomorrow's requirements. Once we are committed to a

computer system and the development of the associated software, it takes considerable time to justify and implement a change. It is therefore incumbent upon us to plan for the solution of tomorrow's problems though they are not totally defined today.

The computer graphics research facility at Lockheed-Georgia has provided a rare opportunity for gaining insight and experience into the vast area of man-computer systems. Familiarization with the problems and the general capability of computer graphics will equip our personnel with the background and training to adjust quickly to new and uncharted areas. Indeed, analogous to the portion of the iceberg that lies beneath the water's surface, there are many more as yet undiscerned applications which lie just beneath the surface of current comprehension.*

It is the role of the systems designer to allow for these uncharted areas so that the company may indeed have a profitable and flexible computer graphics system. Because any computer graphics systems design requires an intimate knowledge of a particular company's methods of doing engineering and research, we would recommend that the systems specification team be headed by company personnel who are very familiar with the day-to-day operation of present design procedures. The systems specification has to provide the link between the computer graphics user, engineering and research personnel, and the actual equipment. The people who head this phase, therefore, have to be highly skilled, farsighted and already familiar with the company's current design techniques, although they do not have to be highly skilled in the complexities of the computer itself. We cannot overstate the importance of the systems specification group's role in the future success of the computer-aided design system.

The systems design phase is, to some extent, the next step *down* the ladder of abstraction. The personnel carrying out this function, in contrast to systems specification function, need to be fully aware of the limitations and capabilities of the computer equipment. They need to be able to devise the most efficient way in which the computer graphics system can provide the information required by the systems specifications. Again, because computer-aided design is a newly developing art, these people need a high degree of technical skill. There is little precedent upon which they can base their decisions.

At this phase of implementation, the requirements of the computer graphics user have to again be considered, since so much of the practical

* Chasen, S. H., "The Introduction of Man-Computer Graphics in the Aerospace Industry," *Proceedings—Spring Joint Computer Conference—1965,* Spartan Books, Inc., Baltimore, 1965.

use of the system depends upon the ease with which the designer can communicate with the machine, while retaining the flexibility he requires. Although it is desirable for the systems design personnel to have a knowledge of the company's actual design procedure, this is not nearly as essential as it is in the case of the systems specifications group. It is thus possible to fill these positions with the best people obtainable, whether from inside or outside the company, although we tend to favor the use of in-house personnel.

The final phase of implementation is the programming. Again, the uncertainty and newness of computer graphics equipment plays a role in the selection of suitable personnel. The programmer's task is more structured than that of either previous case. Nevertheless, it is far more complex and vague than that associated with normal EDP installations. Despite this, top EDP programmers should be capable of adapting to this new task, and consequently personnel from this existing function should be obtained, again either from inside or outside the company.

We are continually faced here with the fact that computer graphics is both new and evolutionary in nature. As such the implementation is an extremely dynamic procedure—dynamic with regard to the development of computer graphics as an art and dynamic with regard to its evolution in a particular company. The requirements of personnel and equipment will change over time. Distinctions between tasks that were once clear will become diffused, and vice versa. We stress the need to view the implementation of a computer-aided design system as a dynamic growing thing; and while we present categories and types of personnel requirements, we emphasize that these distinctions are not static or clearly discernible: their emphasis and scope will change as the computer graphics installation develops. Requirements that may be a necessity today could well be redundant by tomorrow.

This dynamic quality is clearly illustrated when we consider the nature of the personnel required to operate, maintain, and develop the actual computer equipment itself. The state of the art in 1966 suggests that most companies installing computer graphics equipment will require personnel who are highly competent and skilled in computer technology. It sometimes occurs that a particular company's hardware requirements can only be filled by purchasing equipment from a variety of manufacturers. Such equipment must then be interfaced and modified by the purchasing company to suit its own needs. Consequently, it is very important *at this time* that the prospective computer graphics user allow for the inclusion of skilled computer technologists on his computer-aided design staff—the number, of course, varying with the ambitiousness of the project. This requirement, however, will diminish rapidly in the coming years as equipment becomes more stabilized and commonplace.

TECHNICAL DIFFICULTIES

Turning now to the technical difficulties which will have to be surmounted during the development of a computer graphics facility, we feel that these can be classified into three groups: design description, hardware selection, and software compatibility. We do not wish to attempt to solve these difficulties in this report, because their vary nature dictates an intimate knowledge of the actual application for which they are to be used. Rather, our desire is simply to highlight these areas as potential sources of difficulty, for management should be aware of them.

Some of the present limitations of computer graphics revolve around the immense amount of data required to describe and solve a design problem. The whole area of design description assumes increasing importance when it becomes necessary to work consoles at locations remote from the central processor unit. This constraint arises from the need to send vast amounts of information at high speed back and forth between the display unit and the central computer. In addition, the more information required to describe a problem, the larger the computer memory and storage devices needed to handle and process the data. It is clear that the ability to provide condensed design descriptions will have a direct bearing on the speed and cost of operating a computer graphics installation. On a wider basis, this problem of "design description" currently places rather severe restrictions on the type of engineering design problems that can be handled by computer graphics. Most engineering problems have constraints that are many in number and somewhat vaguely defined. Further, many are non-linear. Thus the structuring of problems in a form suitable for use by a computer is a potential barrier that can impede the progress of computer-aided design in many applications. The optimization and simulation techniques that were described in the hypothetical example of the Helverson Manufacturing Company in Chapter I are typical situations that are, as yet, severely limited by the problems of design-description. In fact, after many years of experience with the practical uses of computer graphics on the DAC-I system at General Motors, Donald Hart and Edwin L. Jacks of the General Motors Research Center are convinced that the problems associated with the manipulating, storing, and associating of design data within the computer is one of the major remaining obstacles to the efficient use of computer-aided design.

Work is under way to help solve these difficulties, however, as we have previously noted. Professor B. Herzog of the University of Michigan and Dr. L. Roberts and Douglas Ross of M.I.T., for example, are committed to attacking and overcoming this type of computer graphics limitation. In any event, this difficulty should be raised as a warning flag. The more ambitious the design problem to be solved, the more time consuming and costly it will be; and, in addition, the evidence suggests that the relationship between design problem complexity and time or cost is anything but linear. Rather, we would anticipate it to be more nearly exponential.

The second item on our list of technical difficulties is the question of hardware selection. A background to this problem has been given in previous chapters, and suffice it to say at this point that success is largely in the hands of the technically oriented computer people. However, if a good job has been done in selecting the personnel required to carry out the systems design phase of the project, then realistic hardware requirements should be forthcoming. The only warning we would make is that due consideration be given to the future expansion of the system. It seems almost inevitable that such an expansion will take place, and consequently a careful weighing of the pros and cons of system flexibility and compatibility versus costs could save greatly increased costs at a later date. The economic ramifications of this decision have already been explored in a previous chapter.

The last major technical difficulty is that of software compatibility. The situation associated with computer graphics bears a family resemblance to the problems many companies have faced in their EDP installations. A company's computer operations are often programmed in a computer language that is dependent upon one particular machine. When the time comes to change to a new computer, the company is frequently either locked into either a particular type of machine or forced to reprogram its entire range of computer applications. This can be a very costly procedure as is evidenced, in the case of computer-aided design, for example, by General Motors' need to reprogram its one million 7094 instructions— used with the DAC-I system—in order to convert to a so-called third-generation computer. The point to be made here is that management should satisfy itself that the company's computer-aided design programming effort is the best compromise for both future flexibility and growth in the system and compatibility with a wide range of hardware types. Currently there is little uniformity in the program languages used for computer graphics although the future holds the hope that a general language such as IBM's PL/1 will be further developed to handle these new requirements.

CONTROLLING THE PROCESS

There are two distinct aspects of controlling the computer graphics function in a company. The first, the one we are primarily concerned with here, is the control necessary during the start-up phase, while the second aspect relates to the control exercised on the designer during the actual operating use of the equipment.

The control associated with startup has its objective ensuring that operating usage of the system is obtained in the shortest possible time but not at the expense of long-term benefits. In this regard, the installation of computer graphics is very similar to the installation of an EDP system. In other respects, the difficulties of establishing review and target dates are akin to those of charting any research activity; and because of this, management should be prepared to experience some difficulty in getting the development group to commit itself to deadlines. However, this is something that should and must be done if management is to obtain a return on investment within a predictable period of time. A word of caution is required with regard to drawing too close a comparison between the installation of computer graphics and the installation of an EDP system. The time frame is likely to be completely different, and management must be prepared to expect the payback from the computer-aided design system to be delayed many years.

A useful method of ensuring a payback in a minimum amount of time is through the use of near-term and long-term application groups. By having some of the people responsible for systems specification concentrate on concrete realizable short-term goals, economic as well as morale advantages can be obtained. If the system produces results at an early stage, both management and designers will become committed to the potential worth of the computer graphics effort. As mentioned earlier in this chapter, such a device has been instituted at Lockheed-Georgia and elsewhere with considerable success.

For the start-up stage, we have outlined a broad approach to the evaluation problem, but we have not as yet considered the motivation of the development group. It is our opinion that, provided the computer graphics system has management backing, there will be little need to be concerned about motivation. The people associated with this new technique will be basically doing work of an exploratory nature in an environment associated with research and design; and, if past experience is any guide, the major difficulty will be keeping their sights down, rather than guiding them to look ahead.

At this point it is probably worth re-emphasizing the old adage about "crawling before walking." Management should be constantly on the alert to prevent too grandiose a scheme from pushing the practical worth of the system too far into the future. Evolution not revolution should be the watchword. Overextending one's capability invites disaster. The successes will be to those who understand the size of the job and who plan their activities well.

Turning now to the control of an operating computer graphics system, there are one or two factors that will demand special attention. These relate to the possibility of a designer tying up a console—at considerable cost—and not producing any useful results. The question arises as to how much preparation the designer should have before he comes to the console. Should he have free access to the terminal, or should there be some sort of scheduling or sign-up procedure? Which people should be able to use the facility, and who should be denied access? Should the entire data bank be on call from every console or should safeguards be built in? We have no specific answers to these questions, although we feel that in the long run the best results will probably be achieved by treating the facility as just another piece of laboratory equipment for availability purposes. Whatever procedures the company currently has in force to satisfactorily control the use of engineering facilities will, in our opinion, be transferable with a minimum of modification to the use of graphic consoles. It would probably be advisable to control access to data on the basis of operator codes.

In summary, then, we believe that the major need for careful control procedures will be in the systems specification, systems design and programming phases, rather than in the control of the actual user for any purposes other than security.

THE CRITICAL ROLE OF MANAGEMENT

It seems probable that there will be two dominant attitudes displayed by management towards computer graphics. Some will see it as just another capital investment. Others will see it as something having marked influence upon the total operation of the company. The effects of computer graphics, we believe, will pervade the entire organization, and an investment having this much impact upon the organization demands more than casual involvement. It is important that from the very start *active* management support be gained for the graphics facility; and to emphasize this point, we feel that we can do no better than note a number of comments on this subject.

Professor John Dearden, Harvard Business School, says:

> . . . management has the responsibility for manufacturing an effective information system. It is, perhaps, one of its most important responsibilities. [The manager] cannot avoid this responsibility by delegation. He may, and should, assign the responsibility for implementing the various types of information system that he requires. Nevertheless, these systems are so vital to his ability to function effectively as a manager that he cannot avoid the responsibility for constantly reviewing and evaluating these systems. The more complex and sophisticated the information systems become, the more important this responsibility becomes. And this is true at all levels of management.

John T. Garrity, of McKinsey and Company, put it this way:

> On the basis of our analysis, we conclude that computer-systems success is more heavily dependent on executive leadership than any other factor. No company achieved above-average results without the active participation of top management. And where corporate management in effect abdicated its responsibilities, the results were seldom outstanding.

Finally, M. D. Prince, of Lockheed-Georgia, said:

> Lockheed-Georgia feels that it is succeeding with computer graphics because of top management support, a computer system in a research environment dedicated solely to graphics, and the independent strong programming effort of its group.

A CONCLUDING NOTE

We feel the following factors must be borne in mind when considering computer graphics and the conditions for its success:

- Management commitment to CG from the beginning is *the* most important ingredient of success.
- The initial experimentation and programming of CG is time consuming and expensive.
- The installation phase is critical because it sets the course for the future.
- A CG "champion" is almost a prerequisite for getting the ball rolling.

- The implementation phase of any engineering information system can most conveniently be considered under the following headings: systems specification, systems design, and programming.
- The initial CG installation group should include highly skilled systems specialists, software specialists, and computer hardware technologists.
- The efficient "description" of many design problems is the present major barrier to CG's progress.
- Software flexibility and compatibility is an important ingredient in a continuing CG system.
- Formal control of the CG development group is essential.
- An operating computer graphics system will require several years to develop and will be evolutionary, not revolutionary, in nature.

CHAPTER IX

THE IMPACT OF COMPUTER GRAPHICS
ON THE COMPANY •

THE REPERCUSSIONS within the company of installing a new computer graphics design system in the engineering department are difficult to predict. At this stage in the development of CG there has been no actual experience with the effects of a fully operational system. Nevertheless, by combining a knowledge of the unique qualities of computer graphics with a knowledge of the operational aspects of a modern business, it is possible to make certain predictions concerning the impact of this engineering information system on the organization.

Perhaps the best way to proceed would be to imagine that a complete computer-aided design system has been developed, unknown to the organization, and has been put into operation within the company overnight. Let us assume that complete descriptions of the currently active design projects are on file within the memory devices and that all the necessary operating routines and analysis programs are ready for use. Graphic consoles have been placed throughout the engineering facilities, and the system is capable of performing all the operations depicted in our imaginary Helverson Manufacturing Company. Now we can examine the various parts of the organization and see the impact of the new system on the way it operates internally and in relation to its market and competition.

THE SHORTENED DESIGN CYCLE

One major potential benefit of a computer graphics system is the reduction in time required by the design process. There have been many predictions regarding the magnitude of this reduction, but the interesting fact is that almost without exception the predictions suggest a reduction in the range from 5:1 to 8:1. Since these predictions are the best estimates currently available from informed people, we can foresee very substantial reductions even should, say, only one-half of the predicted magnitude actually materialize.

It can be argued that this reduction will make possible the proposal and testing of more versions of the same product, so that from the end-user's point of view, the major benefit will be one of having more products from which to choose. Whether this does, in fact, turn out to be the case will be determined largely by the actions of competitors. It is our opinion that competition in the marketplace will force a proliferation of many new products and models of existing products and that a trend toward customization will follow the greater use of computer-aided design systems.

It also seems clear that, because of this shortened design cycle, manufacturing concerns using computer graphics will be required to make an increasing number of decisions in any given length of time. This will ultimately affect all functional areas as well as putting a strain on management's ability to meet and to accept continuing change. We can safely state that the greatest impact of CG on the organization will be traceable either directly to the reduction in design cycle time or else to one of the side effects accompanying such a reduction.

MANAGEMENT DECISION MAKING

Considering now, in a more direct manner, the effect of a reduced design cycle upon management decision making, we can clearly see that the area requiring major change will be that of product policy. By taking the rather dramatic example of a reduction in automobile design time of 6:1, it is predictable that management will be extremely hard pressed to formulate decisions quickly enough to direct the new capability for meeting the marketplace. It is a common occurrence in present-day corporate activities to have the design and engineering departments proving to be the bottleneck when it comes to making quick changes in product policy. The advent of a truly operational CG system could easily change this situation to one where either the corporate policy makers or other functional parts of the organization would prove to be the major stumbling blocks to rapid change. In the automobile case cited above, management would need an extremely close link to the marketplace in order to make effective use of this new design flexibility. Market research groups would need to provide continuous warning signals noting changes and trends in consumer tastes, while the sales organization would need to feed back continuous information on competitors' movements. Once a competitor made a move, management would need to evaluate this threat; decide whether to retaliate and, if so, in what way; approve the new investment that might be needed in production and other facilities; approve prototype models; and generally gear up the whole organization to change in the shortest possible time. It would be quite possible for the situation to arise in which some other part of the organization, say, production, would then become the bottleneck blocking rapid change. We feel, however, that in most cases such new bottlenecks would be overcome by the authorization of additional capital investments in those areas, thus providing increased resources necessary to cope with the increased load resulting from the more rapid change.

Returning, for a moment, to the management decision-making function in the automobile example, we can see that management itself may quite easily be faced with the need for a critical self-examination. The time dimension of all information flows will become important. If management is to act, it must have the necessary facts. The installation of a CG system has uncovered a completely new and previously obscured problem. Has the company's information flow been adjusted to meet this new requirement? Was the need to streamline other functional areas foreseen? Were the necessary steps taken to order long lead time equipment such as new machine tools? During the development of CG did management take an active role in highlighting the new critical paths that might develop? In short, has management developed the overall organization to make full use of CG's potential?

Clearly, as we have so often stated, the introduction of CG will be evolutionary in nature and will occur over a period of many years. There is a danger, however, that this evolution, rather than being a blessing that allows management plenty of time to adapt the organization to CG, will become the very factor that tends to lull management into inaction. We tend to believe that this is likely to be the case unless the danger is clearly recognized and positive action is taken to avoid it.

THE IMPACT ON FORMAL ORGANIZATIONAL STRUCTURE

A reduced design cycle implies a faster rate of change. This, in turn, calls for a greater flexibility to adapt. What meaning does this have for formal organization structure?

For purposes of contrast, let us polarize all organizations into two major classes: centralized and decentralized. The former characteristically places emphasis on formal lines of authority with control and profit-making responsibility effectively centered in a central management group. The latter characteristically has been motivated by the desire to push the profit-making responsibility further *down* in the organizational hierarchy. Although this description is a gross oversimplification, it serves its purpose here by conveying the concept of locally autonomous versus centralized modes of operation.

As the need to adapt quickly to change is increased, it would seem that informal communication could become an important ingredient of success. This being the case, one could argue that, on balance, an organization in which responsibility and authority is assigned at lower levels might prove more adaptable to change. Observations on organizational behavior have shown that companies existing in an unstable, fast-changing environment with regard to technical knowledge, function most effectively through an organic organizational structure—that is, one characterized by rather ambiguous job definitions, high interaction rates laterally as well as vertically, and with individuals consciously seeing their own tasks as being performed within the context of the overall task of the firm. This type of behavior is manifested not only in structural differences but also in marked differences in management beliefs, styles of supervision, and the degree of personal involvement felt by the individual towards his work life. It is difficult, of course, to draw anything but the most general of conclusions, but we would hypothesize that, on balance, decentralized organizations, which often exhibit to a greater degree the characteristics just described, will have less difficulty in adjusting to the influence of computer-aided design, than will the often more mechanistically structured centralized organization.

IMPACT ON THE ENGINEERING DEPARTMENT

The engineering department is the area of the company most directly affected by the introduction of the computer-graphics facility. Because the facility will ultimately have some effect on all aspects of design, one can expect to see a considerable change in outlook and emphasis within the design team. We see this change as affecting three main areas: engineering personnel, engineering information flow, and engineering capabilities.

The tasks to be performed by the designer will be somewhat different in nature with the advent of CG. The designer will be freed to solve that part of a design problem requiring an heuristic approach, while the parts that are more easily solved by algorithms will be undertaken by the computer. The more mechanical and routine tasks will eventually find their way into the computer, and the designer will be mainly responsible for applying his abilities to creative thinking. This suggests a new breed of design engineer. The shift will be toward higher educational qualifications with a prime emphasis on the ability to think creatively and solve many unstructured problems.

It will soon become obvious who in the design team is capable of this work. The number of computer hours logged versus the type of problem and the results attained will provide a greater measure of efficiency and comparison among designers than was heretofore possible. The fact that progress with the design will be paced by the designer rather than his tools has the potential of placing a severe strain on him. He will be required to think and to think hard about complex problems most of his working hours. Gone will be the time when the engineer could find some relief by doing a batch of mechanical calculations before attacking the main problem again. The pressure will be on him to match the computer's capabilities.

It is doubtful whether this proposed increase in designer efficiency will reduce the number of designers employed. It will simply mean that they will solve more problems and cover more ground than was previously possible. However, the company will probably experience increasing difficulties in finding and attracting the necessary design talent. This shortage of top-grade men has been apparent in the more technically complex industries for some time, and it will become even more widespread as the acceptance and use of CG raises the level of skill required. The successful designer will need to be trained to use the computer graphics console effectively, as well as to think in terms that complement the computer. The question of designer fatigue occasioned by this high level of interaction is a problem about which we can only surmise at this time. Undoubtedly the designer will find some means of adapting to the increased pressure without losing his ability to think creatively. On this question, Henry Dreyfuss, the country's leading Industrial Designer, commented to us: "There is an untapped reservoir of creativity. A truly creative person becomes even more creative as he works harder."

It is interesting to note that the question of designer education is already being investigated at the University of Michigan, where a course "Industrial

Engineering 591 (Study in Selected I.E. Topics)" is being offered to acquaint and train students in the uses of computers in design. The primary emphasis will be upon computer graphics. The course description reads as follows:

> The feasibility of the effective use of computational and associated aids in research, development, and design has been clearly demonstrated. However, the full potential of the existing methods, and those yet to be developed, has not been explored or employed.

> Engineers, industrial designers, planners, businessmen, and even esthetic designers must be able to use such devices and aids without having to become computer experts. Future developments must strive to achieve this objective.

> This seminar will concentrate on developing a deeper understanding in this most important class of computer applications, whose main purpose is to aid men in processes requiring any degree of creativity.

As we have already implied, the trend in the design department will be away from the performance by designers of the more mechanical techniques. The most obvious area where this will have impact is in the drafting function. Already several papers that discuss the growing concern for the future role of the draftsmen have appeared. The outlook for the drafting function per se is not bright; and because of the social implications involved, we plan to discuss this problem more fully in the last chapter.

As to the second major area of change effecting the engineering department, the engineering information flow, several basic decisions will need to be made during the CG implementation stage. Perhaps the most important and far-reaching concerns the effects of the potential for reducing hard-copy output from the design department. The computer graphics facility presents the dilemma of whether to store drawings in the computer memory devices or to keep the present hard-copy system. Naturally enough, the economics of the situation—memory and storage device costs versus the cost of manual techniques—will contribute substantially to the answer. However, the cost of such devices is continually on the decrease as proposals for more exotic storage facilities come closer to being a reality. The point will be reached when both economically and practically it will be feasible to have all drawing information stored inside the computer for instant recall.

Then the problem will arise of how the information is to be transmitted to other functional areas. In many cases active or passive graphic output devices will suffice, but, for production, hard-copy drawings could be an advantage or even required for certain applications such as those presently requiring undimensioned, scale drawings. This leads us to the question of determining the most pertinent outputs for the production department. At present a batch of drawings and specifications form the basis for information transfers between engineering and the production operation. One must ask, however, whether this is still the most efficient transfer method, once the CG facility is operating.

Dr. Romberg of Arthur D. Little has faced this dilemma in the detailed ship design automation contract with the U.S. Navy. In his Stage-one scheme, the proposal is to include two types of output information. First, he proposes using what he has called "graphic construction aids." These are actual drawings, dimensioned and lettered, prepared on off-line plotters from magnetic tapes. They contrast with present drawings in that there will be more of them for each ship, with less information on each one. The information on each will be that which is required for a particular function: such as cutting or welding. Consequently they will be easier to use and will give rise to less confusion, as they are considerably less cluttered. This increase in the number of drawings is possible because of the relative ease with which a computer can accomplish their preparation. The second output in the Navy system is APT-language programs which, when processed under the APT computer system, will produce tapes capable of driving numerically controlled machine tools. The manufacturing specifications that Dr. Romberg proposes to produce appear equally appropriate for an initial active computer graphics facility.

The advantages of keeping design information within the computer are obvious. In the first place, this means that there is one central location for all drawings, and that a modification or change to the master drawing will instantly change all the "copies." The present problem of working from outdated drawings will be avoided. Second, by keeping the drawing information stored in digital form within the computer, it is a relatively simple matter to drive numerically controlled machine tools directly, either for "hogging out" prototype models, or else for use in the actual production process. Finally, by so storing the information, there has been no forfeiture of the ability to obtain hard copy when required and in the form required. Currently it is possible to use the DAC-I scheme of image processing onto film for projection or printing or else to use plotting machines to draw out—although relatively slowly—full-size prints.

The most serious problems with computer-stored design information involve the protection of this information from destruction or unauthorized disclosure. To be useful, the information must be accessible. Once accessible, however, it becomes subject to change or destruction, unless access is limited to viewing only. We have already noted the use of console-operator identification codes in the DAC-I system. Similar procedural devices, as well as hardware devices such as memory barricades, suggest some solutions.

In weighing the advantages and the problems, it seems clear that the move toward storage of engineering data in computer files will increase. We would also predict that the ultimate success of the CG system will depend upon a satisfactory bridge between the design facility and other functional areas, in particular the production department. The marketing department will, of course, be required to provide last-minute market requirements to the designers.

While considering engineering information flow, we should mention the great advances being made in other types of information retrieval. Lockheed-Georgia is expending considerable effort in supplying its engineers and researchers with the facility for quickly obtaining abstracts of any information published in the field they are researching. The abstracts will be on direct recall through the use of computer graphics. We expect to see a large increase in the usage of this type of information system, especially among the more technical industries where engineers spend a great deal of their time keeping abreast of the new literature.

The final major area of impact upon the engineering function will be the increased ability for carrying out design work. The CG facility will enable the accomplishment of studies that were previously not considered feasible. The Ford Motor Company foresees a great potential in minimizing the "tolerance stackups" that are currently unavoidable when many different designers in different physical locations are developing parts which must mate together. A completely new approach to tolerance allowances both from an assembly and from a manufacturing viewpoint should become feasible. CG will enable designers to try out many more solutions than were previously possible; while, in addition, because the design information is in digital form, it will be possible to quickly produce more three-dimensional mockups than in the past. If one brings down these ideas from generalizations to specific industries or even specific companies, it is possible to find a myriad of applications where CG will make improved design practical. However, this flexibility is, in itself, a danger from the manager's vewpoint. It becomes important to prevent the application of CG to low-return projects. Rather, it must be concentrated in the areas of greatest benefit. This brings home the necessity of ensuring that engineering management and the present engineering control systems are indeed functioning efficiently and that they will continue to perform satisfactorily with the advent of the CG system.

It would appear that ultimately CG will have major repercussions in engineering, especially regarding a designer's qualifications and ability, as well as in the area of information linkage between design and the production and marketing departments. Planning to anticipate these impacts is a key management role.

IMPACT ON OTHER FUNCTIONAL AREAS

We have already discussed in some detail the nature of the change that a CG system will bring to production, especially in terms of the new kinds of manufacturing specifications that will be forthcoming. Additionally, production will be faced with the need for more frequent and more rapid changeovers. It will become increasingly important to utilize truly general-purpose machine tools and other equipment. Numerical control will gain increasing importance, and in operations besides metal cutting. The opportunity to achieve a return on high-cost, special purpose equipment will occur less frequently. It will be necessary for production to plan carefully its flexibility to accommodate change. The pains of changeover should be eased, however, by the more appropriate, useful, and accurate forms in which design information is received from engineering. Startups and reject problems normally associated with new models should be reduced. Once production has adapted to the new way of operating, increased efficiency should result.

The main effect of CG on marketing will be the need to feed back information on the marketplace and competition to engineering far more quickly and continuously than has previously been the case. This in turn implies the need for a more efficient market research organization, as well as an improved decision-making procedure for determining new products and model changes. An increased rate of product change will occur if the market can be expanded thereby or if competition forces it. Initially, the firms with CG will have a potentially better competitive position and could both force the pace and compel other manufacturers to develop the capability. The large amount of time required to bring an operational CG system into being could mean that firms without the facility will be sacrificing a lead time of three to five years to their competitors.

The effect on purchasing is likely to be largely an intensification of the normal problems of locating and managing efficient sources of supply. The logistics problem will be complicated by the increasing demand for a greater variety of materials and services on shorter notice than before. A particularly bothersome problem could arise in regard to subcontractors. The educating of subcontractors in the use of the "new style" manufacturing specifications could be difficult. It might even be necessary to re-examine the basis for subcontracting to determine whether benefits overcome the dampening effect subcontractors could have on achieving the full benefits of CG.

Finance and control, of course, will be very much involved in the economic aspects of the CG decision. It also seems clear that higher product turnover will place greater emphasis on effective cash flow and budget projections. Quick decisions on new investments might lead to a greater than normal number of "investment failures." For this reason, the tendency for the marketplace to take control of product investment decisions will have to be carefully watched by the financial staff. While the production of a greater variety of products might enable the company to keep up with its competitors, the pertinent question which must be answered is whether this proliferation of new designs will, in fact, bring greater sales and hence increased revenue. Obviously if greater changes take place within the company and more capital investments are made for a shorter period of time, the effect on return on investment could be disastrous, unless sales bring increased revenue either through greater volume or increased prices, and unless plant and equipment investments can be made general purpose. The situation resolves itself into a debate over whether the customer can be enticed to turn over the products he buys even more quickly than is presently the case. If this does not prove to be so, a dampening effect that will serve to reduce the emphasis on product proliferation may be encountered; and CG may be more useful for optimizing the basic designs.

The requirements placed on the personnel department will be largely the result of skill shifts in the engineering department. The emphasis in engineering will be toward more creative thinking. Consequently the requirements for draftsmen, tracers, clerks, and those handling the more mechanical tasks will diminish. We anticipate that many industries will find that designers of the caliber they require will be very difficult to secure. This will continue until education becomes geared to accepting and teaching the new skills required by the advent of CG. Although the

University of Michigan is pioneering in this area, we anticipate that there will be a considerable gap between the demand for, and the supply of, adequately trained engineers. Concurrent with this emphasis on the true designer, we expect that there will be a de-emphasis on the technician.

For in-house personnel, the company should give consideration to a sponsored education program that will aim to guide the design team to obtaining maximum use of the facility. This education program could also be expanded to include seminars to explain the operation of CG to the company staff. In this regard Commander Craig of the U.S. Navy, has made concrete steps for gaining commitment from members of his organization to the concept of computer-aided design. Currently, he has held a 24-hour school for supervisors, officers, and managers on present-day computer technology. In addition, he has had six classes—of 40 each—for supervisors. The process of explaining the effect of computer graphics to the company is an important step in removing fears and gaining commitment.

It is pertinent here to consider the effect of CG on overall personnel requirements. It is extremely difficult to generalize and draw any definite conclusions in this area, as each company and industry has its own peculiar set of problems. We would anticipate, however, that the evolutionary development of CG will, initially, cause very little reduction in personnel requirements that could not be handled by normal attrition. As CG becomes more widespread and accepted, significant problems will be encountered with regard to draftsmen. This appears to indicate a potential unheaval of such magnitude that we will leave a full discussion of the problem to a later chapter. Suffice it to say, at this point, that most companies' requirements for routine draftsmen will ultimately dwindle to practically nothing. A secondary and longer-range effect that might affect production workers is related to the degree of automation that CG evokes in the factory. So much has been written on this subject of automation by people such as John Diebold and others, that it is unnecessary for us to add further comments here.

An interesting side effect that might occur in recruiting top engineering personnel is that there will most probably be a certain status afforded to designers who work on CG. Consequently, companies who actively use a CG system could quite possibly attract a better quality engineer than those who have not installed the system. In addition, the morale of the company's design team would be heightened by the fact that their work utilizes the latest advances in technology.

We would, therefore, conclude that high-quality designers will become difficult to obtain as CG upgrades the standards required; that the mere fact of having a CG installation in the company will help attract the better quality designer; that draftsmen and the more mechanical functions of today's engineering laboratories will tend to disappear; and that in-house company education programs will be needed both to educate company designers and also to gain commitment from all supervisory personnel.

THE EXTENT OF CHANGE

If we had to introduce a secretly developed CG system into a company overnight, there is reason to doubt seriously whether it would be worth much. The computer graphics system would be of value only if:

1. The engineers had been prepared to receive it by training and recruitment.
2. Management had been prepared to act rapidly on product decisions.
3. The marketing organization had improved its ability to provide rapid, continuous data on market conditions and competitors' movements.
4. The management information system had been prepared to provide timely, accurate data for management decision making.
5. The organizational structure were such as to facilitate adaptation in a fast-changing environment.
6. The production department had been prepared to receive different, if more appropriate, manufacturing specifications.
7. The plant and equipment were general purpose and not dependent for payback on a static product.
8. Engineering management had been prepared to control effectively the use of the new system.
9. Subcontractors had been replaced by in-house production or had developed the ability to use CG-produced specifications.
10. Finance and control were prepared to provide close watch over cash flows, budget projections, product line profits, and an increased rate of capital investment.
11. Effective plans had been laid for carrying out the personnel changes required.
12. Organizational commitment had been achieved to avoid resistance to the changes.

CHAPTER X

A PLAN OF ACTION •

THE PURPOSE OF THIS BOOK has been to provide the manager with the necessary information on which to base a plan of action for computer graphics in his company. In this chapter we will pull together many of the threads that have run through the preceding parts of the book. The objective is to arrive at a decision. What action should a company take to ensure that it will make the best use of this new tool?

The methodology we will use in this chapter requires some comment. We will first briefly summarize the state of the art. Then we will discuss our expectations concerning future technological developments and their implications for computer graphics usage. These two sections will form the technical basis for the decision. We will proceed to point out the importance of actions by those groups external to the company, such as competitors, the computer manufacturers, government, and educational institutions. With this background we will be able to turn our attention to internal company considerations. The suitability of the company and its industry for computer graphics can be judged, and the need for a feasibility study can be determined. On the basis of all these considerations, one of the three basic alternatives for action can be selected, and the steps for carrying them out can be noted.

In many ways this chapter is a capsule version of the entire book, with the added emphasis now of a plan of action. To have attempted to deal with the question of a plan of action prior to this point, however, would have been premature. Many of the important points made in earlier chapters will necessarily find their way into this chapter only in very summary form. Nevertheless, they form the basis for our conclusions here, even though they cannot be cited in depth.

THE STATE OF THE ART

It has been demonstrated that a design engineer can communicate effectively and usefully with a computer in graphic terms. Passive computer graphics techniques have been found useful and justifiable in a variety of applications to the design process. The greatest value has been in assisting the engineer to "see" better the results of his conceptualization and thus analyze its expected performance and make improvements on that basis. We have seen examples of this in the Boeing pilot visibility studies and aircraft engine removal study. Passive graphics has been most widely used in the specification of the design solution. The Douglas cable-design group, the North American AUTODRAFT system, and Dr. Romberg's detailed ship design system are examples. Passive graphics techniques are useful so long as hard-copy media for the storage and communication of the design are required, and this will be the case for many years.

It has been demonstrated that a design engineer can communicate with a computer in graphic terms in real-time both under conditions of full-time service of the console by the computer and under multiprogramming operation wherein the console is serviced on an interrupt basis. Active computer graphics has been shown to be useful for drawing, assisted by powerful aids, and for analyzing designs as to expected performance. These capabilities have been proved at the M.I.T. Lincoln Laboratory, the General Motors Research Center, and the Lockheed-Georgia Research Center. It has been shown that design engineers can learn to use the equipment with, at the very least, no more difficulty than was involved in learning to use the computer under more traditional conditions.

It has been shown that the designer can operate effectively in an interactive fashion in conjunction with the computer. Significantly more rapid convergence on design solutions has occurred. Active graphics has proved beneficial in many ways difficult to quantify, but specific reductions in element design time and in parts programming time have been achieved in the range of 5:1 to 10:1. Very realistic estimates of reductions as high as 17:1 in other applications have been confidently forecasted by current users.

We have seen the high costs associated with developing the required software. However, we have seen that the cost of currently available equipment, even when burdened to amortize the cost of software development and when allocated on a full-cost basis to consoles engaged in design applications, results in a cost per console per hour that is in line with the kinds of savings being experienced. Intangible benefits serve materially to enhance the economic attractiveness of active graphics systems.

A number of technical developments are important to realization of the full potential of computer graphics. We have discussed them at a number of points, but here we would like to consider the probable timing as to when these developments can be expected to occur.

IMPORTANT TECHNICAL DEVELOPMENTS

The technical developments, to be discussed, will affect decisions with regard to computer graphics on three counts. First, they will provide for very substantial decreases in the cost of developing a CG capability and of operating such a facility. Second, they will determine just what applications are actually technically feasible. Third, the timing of their occurrence will dictate the rate at which CG is adopted and used. Beyond the initial feasibility study, the economics of CG revolve around the cost of specific applications. As costs decrease and new applications become technically feasible, the decisions to develop and use these new applications will become economically justifiable.

Time-sharing, we have seen, is critical to the full development of computer-aided design systems based on computer graphics. Multiprogramming permits economical operation of a few consoles but presumes the use of batch-processed "background" operation to help support the costs of the installation. Response times under multiprogrammed operation become marginal rather quickly as the number of consoles increases. This is the result of the need to service each interrupt to a logical stopping point. Time-sharing promises more rapid response to a larger number of consoles through the use of efficient scheduling algorithms. The hardware and software associated with time-sharing are fairly well advanced. M.I.T.'s Project MAC and the Dartmouth-General Electric system are in operation and are receiving extensive use. Time-sharing on third-generation computers is scheduled for availability in 1968. Given the kinds of lead time being experienced in the computer industry, one needs to order now for delivery in 1968 anyway; so that for planning purposes, time-sharing can be said to be here today.

Time-sharing is, indeed, here today in a slightly different sense: that is in the form of the computer utility. The first operational utility was reported as follows:

> . . . the nation's first business information utility, Keydata Corp., began operation in Cambridge, Mass., last week [December 1, 1965].

> Keydata went on line to 20 customers in the Boston area. Users pay about $1,000 a month to plug into the company's information service via private telephone lines. The customers include a liquor distributor, a book publisher, and a dozen or so other companies that are mainly interested in invoicing and inventory control.

> The Company's Univac 491 cranks out invoices and bills and calculations on a real-time, or instant-response basis. Its capacity is more than 200 simultaneous users, and the system can easily be expanded. William F. Emmons, Jr., executive vice president, says that Keydata expects to serve New York by the end of the first quarter of 1966 and "eventually cover the United States."[1]

The emergence of the computer utility bears promise for larger companies as a device to supplement in-house capacity temporarily, or even permanently for certain kinds of service. For the small company, it is a very significant breakthrough. It suggests that even small companies will be able to have access to the power of a large computer (such as CG requires) even though they may only be able to support a few consoles.

Western Union has announced plans for computer utility operations on limited applications in the 1970's. It is our opinion that many small companies will be able to use active computer graphics on relatively unstructured kinds of design problems (of the sort requiring a high degree of man-machine interaction) by 1975.

A technological development which bears directly on the economics of computer graphics is the continuing trend toward lower-cost memories. We are not concerned here with an exact definition of memory except that it is the means by which information is retained in a reasonably accessible form in the computer. For our purposes, memory may include core, disk, drum, tape—or newer, more exotic types. IBM now offers about three times as much memory capacity in the form of disk packs as it did a few years ago for the same price. More information can now be stored on a magnetic tape by a factor of about eight over what was possible a few years ago. Such reduced storage costs are the result of new technology, new production techniques, and competition. These same

[1] "Computer Time-Sharing Goes on the Market," *Business Week,* December 4, 1965, p. 116. Used by permission.

factors will serve to continue the trend toward lower cost memories. John Diebold has predicted that information storage in a computer system will be possible on a type of film chip with a drop in the cost per character stored from one dollar to four-tenths of a cent by 1973.[2] In order to store design descriptions in sufficient detail to support a fully developed computer graphics systems, large memories are required. Lower-cost memories will make such an application even more attractive.

A wide variety of software developments will serve to accelerate the development of large-scale CG systems. Traditional higher-level language compilers must provide graphical input-output programming capability. At this point in time, no such capability is to our knowledge being planned, by the computer manufacturers, but such capabilities will be necessarily forthcoming. Monitors or operating systems must provide for graphical console servicing. According to IBM, the Operating System/360 will be extended by August 1966 to provide for the servicing, in batch mode, of one or more 2250 Model I consoles, on all configurations from Model 30 up. In April 1967, extensions to Operating System/360 will have been made to handle multiple 2250's in a multiprogramming environment. By September 1967, the System 360/67 will be able to serve multiple consoles on a fully time-shared basis.

We have noted the advancements in list processing and data management that are needed to permit extensive analyses and design simulations to be conducted. The several well-staffed groups that are working on such problems can be expected to provide meaningful results within a few years. A number of very good systems exist today, and advances are occurring regularly. We fully expect to see schemes developed that will solve the bulk of the problems at least by 1970.

The use of the graphic console itself for programming bears great promise, but this development will probably not be a reality for a number of years. Compilers that will accept as program input flow charts drawn on the scope face are the subject of research at the Computer-Aided Design Project at M.I.T. We do not foresee useful results before 1970.

Developments in computer graphics hardware will also accelerate the development of large-scale CG systems. Improved passive graphics equipment including image processors; high-speed, high-precision hard-copy plotters; and microfilm storage for inactive design files will be forthcoming. Active graphics hardware with improved display size, resolution, and stability will also be forthcoming. The cost of graphic consoles will decrease as more

[2] Diebold, John, "What's Ahead in Information Technology," *Harvard Business Review,* September-October 1965, p. 80.

equipment manufacturers add them to their line, and as volume production permits economies. We expect to see constant improvement in the hardware associated with CG over the next decade. Equipment now available permits most kinds of applications to be implemented. Improved equipment will permit faster, more accurate off-line input-output of graphical information and the ability to perform more accurate free-form drawing on-line on the scope face.

To assist in the process of free-form drawing, improvements are needed in free-form surface definition. The aerospace industry has been able to express aerodynamic surfaces mathematically for some time. Surfaces, such as those encountered in automobile styling, are more difficult to define. Encouraging advances have been made in this regard by Professor S. A. Coons at M.I.T., who has demonstrated the feasibility of general surface definition based on a general and flexible surface equation. This technique has been used to develop defined surfaces which can then be "massaged" into shape by use of a light pen. On the basis of such developments, we foresee general-purpose, precise surface definitions by 1970.

All of the technological developments we have been discussing will be important to computer graphics. We foresee most of the technical problems solved by 1970. The further development of computer utilities will bring CG into the small company by 1975. From the technical point of view, then, computer graphics is a topic for serious planning and action by large companies today. For small companies, the day is not far off when they, too, will need to deal seriously with this development. We noted that for some heavily engineering-oriented small companies, CG is also a topic for action today.

EVENTS IN THE BUSINESS ENVIRONMENT

Technological developments are only one element in the complex picture that must be evaluated in order to reach a decision with regard to CG. Actions taken in several areas of the business environment will affect any given company's position.

The most important segment of the environment to be watched for action is the company's competition. Should a competitor develop a computer graphics system unchallenged, he would have a significant advantage in design time and cost. For this reason a very fundamental decision must be made quite early. Will it be advantageous to go slowly, in the hope of capitalizing on whatever results our competitors attain, or would it be preferable to seize the initiative? There are sound arguments either way, and they tend to resolve into an assessment of the risks of spending large amounts of money, only to lose the advantage, versus the risk of not being able to overcome a competitor's lead quickly. This decision is fundamental to the company's philosophy and competitive strategy and can only be mentioned here. We tend to feel, however, that the very far-reaching implications a CG system has for all aspects of a company's business are such as to require an assimilation over time. It may not be possible to move as quickly as required by a "follower" strategy.

The *computer manufacturers* will play an important role in determining the rate at which computer graphics develops. Should they actively promote CG hardware, and back up their promotion with various kinds of support, it may be desirable to enter into cooperative ventures in conjunction with them. We have seen the role the computer manufacturer has played in the General Motors DAC-I system, and the same is true of other current efforts. By jointly developing the system, it is possible to influence the manner in which the manufacturer designs his proprietary line. Such influence could be beneficial to the company concerned, since its own special problems can be taken into account.

In any case, a close watch must be kept on the computer manufacturers to monitor hardware and software developments. Of special importance would be standard operating subroutines which might be made available and which could significantly reduce the cost of in-house software development. An example would be a two-dimensional drawing package, which most new users would want, and which would serve as a marketing aid for the manufacturer.

For any company engaged in government contracting, the attitude of government agencies can be an indicator of the importance attached to computer graphics. We have noted the U.S. Navy Computer-Aided Design Project under Commander Donald Craig. The U.S. Air Force has, since its inception, been a major supporter of the M.I.T. Computer-Aided Design Project as well as associated projects at the Air Force Cambridge Research Laboratories and the M.I.T. Lincoln Laboratories. The National Aeronautics and Space Administration has demonstrated its interest by such action as the support they have given the authors. This representative listing suggests the importance many defense-related agencies attach to CG. The implications for contract bidding are clear.

Educational institutions are another class of interested party which needs to be watched for action. We have described the University of

Michigan activities under Professor Bertram Herzog. M.I.T. has taken formal notice of its relationship with industry as follows:

> An important goal of the Computer-Aided Design Project is the dissemination of information generated by the group to interested users outside M.I.T. During the past year, it was our pleasure to have, as guests of the Laboratory and Project MAC, seven systems programmers from industry. Our guests have participated in the development of the various programming systems described above and plan to apply and expand further the basic concepts embodied in them upon return to their respective organizations. This program of cooperative research and development with visiting staff from industry will continue as an important aspect of the Laboratory's work in computer-aided design.[3]

As a source of knowledge, working experience with the systems, and trained people, the educational institutions are difficult to equal. They provide a prime source for a "champion" of computer graphics.

Actions taken by any of these areas of the business environment—competitors, computer manufacturers, government agencies, or educational institutions—can affect the context within which a company decision regarding CG must be made. Educational institutions and computer manufacturers are sources of knowledge and assistance in undertaking a CG system implementation. Government and competitors are sources of pressure for developing a system.

INTERNAL CONSIDERATIONS

The state of the art may dictate what is possible today, expectations for new technological developments may influence the timing of action, and the environment may be the source of both help and pressure; but the appropriateness of computer graphics for any company can only be judged by an appraisal of internal considerations. We have seen the important industry and company characteristics which indicate the potential for beneficial use of CG in design. Large engineering-oriented companies designing and producing complex, multiple-system projects subject to rapid change and pressures for high performance are the most likely candidates. The areospace, automobile, shipbuilding, electrical and electronics industries, as well as others, have these characteristics. Some smaller companies whose primary competences are in design are also likely candidates. Size and financial strength are characteristic of those companies pursuing a

---

[3] *Annual Report, 1964-1965,* Electronic Systems Laboratory, Department of Electrical Engineering, Massachusetts Institute of Technology, pp. 26-27.

long-term program toward a full-fledged CG system. More limited applications are appropriate for smaller companies. In either case computer expertise and management commitment to change are necessary ingredients.

THE FIRST DECISION

It is possible to make an initial decision. Either computer graphics is not *now* important to a company and not likely to *become* important to it, or it merits further study. In the former case the investigation is complete. In the latter case it is time for a feasibility study. Such a feasibility study would have the purpose of considering more closely the economics of CG in the company in order to recommend action with regard to the equipment, staffing, training, and the scope and timing of implementation. An approach to the economic considerations was developed in a previous chapter and is recommended as a guideline for the feasibility study. The necessary conditions for successful implementation and some assessments of the organizational and operational implications have also been made. This information, in conjunction with the timing of technological developments that we projected above, can form the basis for decisions on matters of timing of implementation and of organizing to carry out the development task.

THE SECOND DECISION

We foresee three possible outcomes as a result of the feasibility study. First, there is the possibility that, for whatever reason, no commitment can be made at this time but that it is important to stay aware of developments for a later re-evaluation. Second, it may be decided that it is desirable to develop the basic in-house technical skills and gain some operating experience while limiting the amount of committed funds to as small an amount as possible. Third, it may be apparent that CG represents a unique opportunity for improvement of company performance and that it is desirable to capitalize on the opportunity as rapidly as possible.

In the first case, of making no commitment but staying aware of developments, it is important to identify sources of information, and then to monitor them. The technical literature, users, and universities are the best sources. Two or three well-qualified technical people should be designated for this task on a part-time basis. Successful monitoring, however, also requires that management be continually aware of significant developments in order to determine the point at which a larger-scale re-evaluation of the company's position is required. For this purpose, the monitoring group should be required to submit periodic reports and appraisals of recent developments.

The second case, in which it is desirable to develop the basic in-house technical skills to gain some operating experience while limiting the amount of committed funds, is best served by acquiring a small active graphics facility. A console operated in a multiprogramming mode from an existing large-scale computer is probably the best solution. A team of ten to twenty systems designers and programmers would be required. The objectives of this experimental facility must be very carefully defined. It would be very easy to expend funds and achieve no useful results. For this reason, the activities of an experimental facility should be defined as the result of studies conducted by a systems specification group. The purpose would be to insure that the projects undertaken by the experimental group, and any programming done by it, would be of value in an expanded future program. The experimental group would, preferably, not be required to demonstrate payback of their costs; rather, their funding should be treated as a research and development expenditure. This group, too, as in the first case above, should remain up to date on new developments.

The third case, in which it is desired to capitalize on CG as rapidly as possible, requires a much broader plan of action. In its initial stages, this plan would resemble the plan proposed for the second case. Some basic hardware should be acquired, and a team of systems designers and programmers should be assembled. In this case, however, the systems specification group should be devoting full-time effort to defining the application packages to be developed. It would be advisable to define separate near-term and long-term activities.

For the near term, the objective would be to implement the easier application packages in order to put the project on a paying basis. A two-dimensional drawing package, the modification of existing analysis programs to accept graphic, on-line input and output, and a numerical control graphic parts programming package are promising examples. As such packages are developed, they should be placed into the hands of the engineering departments concerned, after proper training. The computer graphics hardware should be planned for expansion as the packages become available and are put to use. As soon as the volume of use justifies it, time-sharing operation should replace multiprogramming operation. It is important, therefore, that the original hardware selected and software developed be amenable to easy transfer to larger configurations.

The long-term objective would be to define, as completely as possible, the ultimate system desired. This activity is best carried out by the systems specification group. This ultimate system would serve as the basis on which hardware plans would be laid and on which near-term programming systems design would be based. One of the most important objectives of this activity would be to define the impact the ultimate system would have on the whole organization. On the basis of this study, important plans would be made for preparing the organization for the changes that would be necessary in order to realize fully the potential benefits of a full-fledged computer-aided design system. We have seen the important ramifications for production, purchasing, marketing, finance and control, personnel, and company management. The most rapid progress can occur only when action has been taken to prepare the way for the necessary changes.

All three of the alternative courses of action described here require management commitment and intelligent management action. We have described what is possible. *The responsibility ultimately falls on management to make it happen.*

CHAPTER XI

A LOOK AT THE FUTURE OF
COMPUTER GRAPHICS •

THIS CHAPTER will be devoted to discussing some future developments involving computer graphics. The very nature of the subject matter will lead us to "blue sky" predictions. The objective of this chapter is not to obtain a 100-percent accuracy rating. Rather it is to dream a little, and from this to point out what we consider to be likely developments which may take place anywhere up to 20 to 30 years into the future. All the implications these developments might have for the businessman would be difficult to discern. Perhaps discussing them will act as a catalyst to spark off other ideas and uses for computer graphics; perhaps we will indicate future business possibilities—we leave it to the imagination of the reader. We feel, however, that any prediction regarding a major change in today's concept of a business organization is worthy of consideration.

From this point on, we take the liberty of enlarging the specialized definition of computer graphics that was proposed in Chapter I. Now, when we speak of computer graphics, we will mean the complete field of graphical communication with a computer, *whether it be applied to product design or not*. We make this change to allow ourselves to range over broader fields in predicting future developments.

We have already mentioned a revolution which will begin to take effect within the next ten years: the computer utility. In its most advanced form, the computer utility would be likened to the present nationwide telephone system. When such a utility is functioning, it will be possible for any firm to rent a connection to what is in effect a gigantic central computer. To make use of this machine, the potential user will simply plug his input-output devices into a connection in the wall. He will then have access to the computer and be charged *only* for the time that he is actually using the central processor of the main unit. This is, in effect, a large central time-shared computer.

The days of individual company selection of a computer would be numbered. A business will simply rent a line and it will effectively have its own computer. While this utility concept may overcome hardware problems, it will certainly still leave the major management headache of systems design and programming with the company using the facility. From the computer-aided design aspect, the company, by merely acquiring the graphic consoles, will have hardware immediately operational. This means that, once this utility becomes available, even the smallest factory owner will be able to use an automated design system. Further, major companies will be able to relay the appropriate design information to subcontractors, and so one need for hard-copy drawings will have been eliminated.

When considering this utility concept, an interesting problem comes to mind. This is the possibility that one company, in some manner or other, will gain access to another company's design information. Such doubts regarding security of proprietary information will need to be clearly resolved before the concept of the utility will become universally acceptable.

At present one of the limiting factors of CG is the restriction of the display to two-dimensional representations. This limitation is overcome to some extent by rotating the display and thus creating the illusion of 3-D. We feel, however, that true 3-D presentations upon the screen will become a must for the future. This observation is predicated upon the fact that for many product design purposes, such as styling, 3-D is an essential ingredient. Currently, the solution seems to be by either of two methods. First, a return to the principles used in three-dimensional movies could be made. In these movies there were two screens which had slightly different angle views of the same object, and by the use of red-green spectacles or some form of polarized light, it was possible to create the illusion of three dimensions. The other possible solution might be with the Hologram. This is a device developed at the University of Michigan by Professor G. W. Stroke and basically is the formation of three-dimensional objects through the exposure of a photo-sensitive surface to laser beams. Recent news articles point to the possibility of using the device for both television and movie 3-D applications.[1] It is our opinion that Holography will eventually be the technique that provides an effective three-dimensional color display for computer graphics. In any event, the demand for 3-D displays—especially among the automobile and industrial designers—will eventually bring about the availability of such a feature. Color displays are available, in theory, at the present time, and it needs only the creation of sufficient demand for them to become a reality. One will have to pay the penalty of increased costs and programming complexity, however, in order to accept color and 3-D.

A third major advance of computer graphics will be in the field of computer programming. At present, the difficulties in programming unstructured design problems are immense. We have already touched on this in earlier chapters, but a more detailed discussion is now called for.

It is, of course, already possible to program specific problems, but it is an extremely complex task to generalize a program in order to treat large classes of problems. This difficulty is currently being attacked at M.I.T., where efforts are being made to produce a generalized programming scheme. The approach is to seek a set of "computational atoms" with which one could construct a useful analytical capability for any given design at any given time. A parallel can be found in Euclid's postulates in geometry, whereby a set of basic building blocks can be connected together in various ways to obtain a wide variety of results. Similarly, in the M.I.T. approach to programming, the designer can connect these generalized building blocks in order to perform the design function that he wishes. In the ultimate system, the computer will be programmed by way of the scope face. The designer will actually use the computer graphics console to construct a program based on building blocks. The availability of this powerful technique will be instrumental in increasing the usefulness of computer graphics in the solution of unstructured design problems. In addition, it will revolutionize computer programming, whatever the application.

POTENTIAL AREAS FOR THE USE OF COMPUTER GRAPHICS

The potential areas in which computer graphics might be used in the future are really only limited by the imagination. We will, however, present several of our predictions here.

First, we see great advances possible in the use of computer graphics

[1] *Wall Street Journal,* March 7, 1966, and *Time,* March 18, 1966.

as a teaching device. Students learning mathematics, for instance, could have visual presentations of the graphical form of mathematical equations. As the student defines changes in various coefficients, the computer would display the resulting effect on the screen. Use of these devices as a teaching aid has already been made by Professor A. G. Oettinger, Professor of Applied Mathematics at Harvard University. In a seminar entitled "Technological Aids to Creative Thought," Professor Oettinger is studying the problems of teaching mathematics. We can visualize similar applications in economic model building and in physics. In the latter, for example, the effect of changes in the damping factor upon harmonic oscillations could easily be displayed for instantaneous viewing on the screen. The student would quickly be able to see the result of change, rather than, as at present, being required to wade through masses of repetitious calculations and curve plotting.

Professor B. F. Skinner, also of Harvard, has spent considerable time developing the teaching machine for programmed learning as a means of improving the learning process for many students. A CG display console would provide an excellent device for this application, so much so that we can foresee the decline of the mechanical teaching machine in all major programmed learning centers. One can even foresee the advent of the computer utility and computer graphics allowing students to take courses in the home. A combination of lectures and programmed instruction could be obtained through the rental of a display unit that could be connected to the home telephone line or its equivalent. Access to the teaching material stored in a central computer would be controlled by some form of security device. The work of Professors Oettinger and Skinner, combined with the use of CG, would thus open up a new era of truly individualized teaching.

Another potential area for the use of computer graphics is in the hospital. One can imagine a portable display being wheeled from patient to patient in the wards. The doctor could call up the patient's medical records and view both the printed word and the charts. Inputs could be made regarding prescriptions to be ordered from the pharmacy, reservations for surgery, and so on. Its form would be very similar to IBM's Hospital Information System with the added capability of receiving the results of laboratory tests, viewing medical records, and so forth instantaneously and visually on a screen.

Another area is the most unlikely field of cartoon animation. The computer graphics console offers great potential for rapid and inexpensive production of cartoons. Having outlined the original scene and the major positions assumed by the characters during the episode, it becomes a simple matter to create the many intermediate drawings which are required for smooth-flowing movement but which represent a time-consuming chore for the animators. The mathematical techniques exist today for creating incremental, smooth-flowing positions once the end points are defined. Already serious attention is being paid to this possibility by some film makers.

Turning to yet another application, we foresee an impact on the dress designing and fashion business, and in fact, on the whole garment industry. By sketching a new design on the screen, it would eventually be possible, through the use of 3-D, for the fashion designer to, in effect, walk around his new creation. Having finalized the details, the computer would then sketch out the material cutting patterns, as well as calculate all the dimension changes required by the various sizes. One further stage of sophistication would be to then have the computer control the cloth cutting knives. The first steps in this direction have already been taken by the Catalina division of Kayser-Roth Corporation.[2] Using an ordinary computer with a curve plotter, designers develop the various sizes of swimsuits from the original standard-size model. This technique promises considerable time savings in an industry where timeliness is critical.

A major field of interest to management is the potential use of computer graphics in management information systems, and also in simulation or model building. The application to management information systems suggests the use of display consoles to allow operating management to call up information instantaneously from a computer-stored data bank. Financial statements, correspondence, market forecasts, or historical information could be available. The role of the display in this case is largely one of information retrieval. Aside from business, we expect even greater impact of such a facility in fields such as law, medicine, and government where rapid access to large volumes of up-to-date and historical information is an important capability for the discipline concerned. Very promising progress is already being made in such applications.

In the field of simulation or model building we see the graphic console becoming a very useful tool. The simulation of inventory, production, and marketing systems has all the well-known features of allowing the effects of system changes to be seen at a minimum cost. The use of CG should enhance the ease with which such models are designed, tested, implemented, and used. Techniques such as M.I.T. Professor Jay For-

[2] *Business Week*, October 16, 1965.

rester's Industrial Dynamics[3] are obvious examples of suitable applications. Many forms of non-engineering analysis require the use of graphics. One tool used in statistics, for example, is correlation and regression analysis. This is a method used to define the relationship between variables in situations where causal relationships are not clear or don't exist in a definable way, and where experimental methods are not satisfactory. Curves are fitted to plots of observed data in order to define the relationship in a useful form. Fitting the curve to satisfy the least mean square test is an iterative process using graphics. If the proposed curve could be drawn on a console display of the data, with the computer performing the variance computation, the process would be greatly facilitated. Similar applications suggest themselves in a host of nonengineering fields.

These, very briefly then, are several glimpses of potential uses of computer graphics which could very likely be commonplace in the world of tomorrow. It can be seen that the implications of computer graphics can and will be far-reaching. Just as automation of production facilities is today causing considerable social upheaval and change, we see this next major advance of "automation" by computer graphics causing a similar social impact. In addition, the ability of the business organization to create even more rapid technological change will in turn place additional emphasis on the question of a company's social responsibility to the community. Further, we have described how some of the technical and economic barriers blocking the widespread usage of computer graphics will be overcome, and how this progress will open up unlimited possibilities of applying these new techniques to a broad range of current problems.

In the light of the foregoing, we feel justified in predicting a meaningful future for the application of computer graphics to the business organization. As with all new techniques, the initial evolution of the tools will be slow, but we would stress that computer-aided design is one of the most technically and conceptually complex tools to face management since the introduction of electronic data processing. As a corollary to this, we predict that the time required to develop even a small computer-aided design facility will be several years for most firms. Management should give serious consideration *now* to investigating the meaning of computer graphics for their firm, even if applications appear to be five to ten years away. The complexity and far-reaching effect upon the organization of this technique point to the wisdom of early action.

[3] Forrester, Jay W., "Industrial Dynamics—A Major Breakthrough for Decision Makers," *Harvard Business Review,* July-August 1958.

THE IMPACT OF COMPUTER DESIGN ON SOCIETY

A major study was recently undertaken by the U.S. Department of Labor.[4] Among other things, this report concludes that by 1975 there will be no drastic change in the total number of draftsmen in the labor force because, although the occupational growth rate will be slower, the total number will still increase. It contends that the least affected will be those working on dimensioned drawings, such as are used in complex mechanical design. However, it does state that in the following ten-year period, 1975 to 1985, there could be a drastic reduction in draftsmen as the widespread use of time-sharing comes about. The report also maintains that the only foreseeable impact of any consequence upon the designer-draftsman within the ten years from 1965 on will be the advent of computer graphics. The reason given for the adoption of this or any other technological change in the design field is not the reduction of labor costs but the reduction of lead time and the ability to design the most advanced product for the least cost.

This report suggests that major changes will occur in the draftsmen-designer occupations, although it does not specify exactly when. The best estimate appears to be some time after 1975. This potential displacement of a good number of white-collar workers leads to the question of white-collar worker unionization. (1965 statistics show that there are about 200,000 draftsmen spending almost full time on design-drafting, while nearly 650,000 engineers currently spend 20 percent of their time on design-drafting.) There is considerable feeling in the country that changes in technology will lead to a greater move towards unionization of white-collar workers as expressed by Richard E. Walton.[5] Another report on this subject, particularly directed at the effects of computer-aided design, has been made by Jerome I. Weiner of M.I.T.[6] He advocates the planning of re-education programs for the personnel displaced by computer-aided design, particularly with reference to draftsmen.

The effects we can expect, then, are clear. Because of the use of computer-aided design, we can expect a growing redundancy among engineering white-collar workers. This redundancy will be an important factor in

[4] *Technology and Manpower in Design/Drafting 1965-1975*, Manpower Administration, U.S. Department of Labor, Government Printing Office, May 1966.
[5] Walton, Richard E., *The Impact of the Professional Engineering Union*, Division of Research, Harvard Graduate School of Business Administration, Boston, 1961.
[6] Weiner, Jerome I., "The Impact of Technological Change on Design," Unpublished Notes, Massachusetts Institute of Technology, 1965.

fostering the unionization of this class of worker. Management can expect the demands of such unions to act as a hindrance to the easy acceptance of computer-aided design. However, this movement is not likely to be felt until after 1975.

We would expect that the main impact of computer-aided design on society, however, will result from product proliferation. The effect of competition in the marketplace, and the growing use of planned product obsolescence, will increase the pressure upon the consumer to keep up with the Joneses—and upon society to keep up with the problem of scrap disposal! The proliferation of products might ultimately lead to a virtual customizing of the products of some industries, with the customer being able to choose his own specially designed product. Although it is most likely that the product would belong to a common generic family, many varieties of styling and many optional features would be available. This would be akin to the present trend in the automobile industry, wherein it is possible to more or less customize one's new car by specifying a particular combination of the many options. We see this trend spreading and becoming more pronounced. Such a prediction seems to be consistent with human nature, since the appeal of a unique object appears to be irresistible to most people—perhaps it provides a sense of identity.

There is a negative side to this product proliferation, however. Product proliferation and planned obsolescence may serve to strengthen the feeling that all things are impermanent, and, in a rather intangible way, this could have serious sociological repercussions. Already the rapid rate of change and lack of permanency in our society is giving rise to increasing instability. Computer-aided design, by fostering product proliferation, could serve to reinforce this trend.

This same increased pressure, mentioned above with regard to the buying habits of the consumer, will also come to bear on the designer. He will be called on to produce more products in less time than is currently the case. How important this will be, and how it might effect the creative ability of a true designer, is problematical. We might hypothesize that in order to give the designer an opportunity to "recharge" his creativity, there will be an increase in his vacation time, with perhaps two or three vacation periods a year becoming the norm. Some of this "vacation" time will most probably be spent back at school, where the designer will be attempting to update himself on the burgeoning volume of knowledge that will grow even in his own specialized field.

These, then, are some of the effects that we can expect society to experience as a result of computer-aided design. To reiterate, we see a growing trend towards customization. We believe that the designer, as a subset of society, will be subject to growing pressure and will also need to renew both his creativity and his education much more regularly than in the past. There is little doubt that such aspects as increased leisure time, product proliferation, and the considerable technological change resulting from the adoption of computer-aided design will give rise to their own measure of social change. The question of social responsibility must then be raised; and if a social responsibility is recognized, management should consider how it can act to make this impact a constructive one. As Professor Robert W. Austin, of the Harvard Business School, has said:

> The true responsibility of business leadership is to make some appraisal of the social effects flowing from its strategic policy decisions and technological advances. This is its clear responsibility. It can no longer, as the top management of business, be interested only in its own growth and development. It must expand its responsibility to include awareness of the social changes it creates. Having made some judgment as to the social effects of its activities, business must then make the effort to think beyond the economic and see what kind of action should be taken and by whom to meet the problems of social change.[7]

[7] Austin, Robert W., "Responsibility for Social Change," *Harvard Business Review,* July-August, 1965.

BIBLIOGRAPHY

BOOKS

Bierman, Harold, and Seymour Smidt, *The Capital Budgeting Decision*, The Macmillan Company, New York, 1960.

Diebold, John, *Beyond Automation*, McGraw-Hill Book Company, New York, 1960.

Fetter, William A., *Computer Graphics in Communication*, Engineering Graphics Monograph Series, McGraw-Hill Book Company, New York, 1965.

Hunt, Pearson, *Financial Analysis in Capital Budgeting*, Graduate School of Business Administration, Harvard University, Boston, 1965.

ARTICLES

Austin, Robert W., "Responsibility for Social Change," *Harvard Business Review*, July-August 1965.

"Automatic Drafting Systems," *Mechanical Engineering*, January 1965.

Buck, Gilbert, "The Boundless Age of the Computer" (4 parts), *Fortune*, March to June 1964.

"Computer Can Plan Building in Minutes," *Iron Age*, May 24, 1962.

"Computer Designs Missile Cables," *Steel*, May 10, 1965.

"Computer Frees Engineers to Think Big," *Steel*, December 10, 1962.

"Computer Time-Sharing Goes on the Market," *Business Week*, December 4, 1965.

"Computer Uses 'Logic' to Direct Engineering," *Iron Age*, March 18, 1965.

"Computers Add an Apprehensive New Client," *Fortune*, February 1965.

"Computers Speed the Design Cycle," *Business Week*, November 7, 1964.

"Computers That Feed Many Mouths," *Business Week*, February 1, 1964.

Corbin, Harold S., "A Survey of CRT Display Consoles," *Control Engineering*, December 1965.

Diebold, John, "What's Ahead in Information Technology," *Harvard Business Review*, September-October 1965.

"Draftsmen with Speed to Spare," *Business Week*, May 29, 1965.

"Finding New Ways to Make Autos," *Business Week*, September 11, 1965.

"Ford First to Confirm Diemaking NC," *Control Engineering*, February 1966.

French, Wendell L., "White-Collar Discontents; Symptoms and Solutions," *Management Review*, July 1960.

"From Clay . . . To Tape . . . To Die—A Revolution Comes to Diemaking," *Steel*, July 20, 1964.

Gomolak, L. S., "Better and Faster Design by Machine, "*Electronics,* June 1, 1964.

Harris, William B., "Detroit Shoots the Works," *Fortune,* June 1959.

Hertz, David B., "Risk Analysis in Capital Investment," *Harvard Business Review,* January-February 1964.

Holstein, David, "You and Your Computer," *Product Engineering,* July 20, 1964.

————, "Are You Ready for Computer-Aided Design?" *Product Engineering,* November 23, 1964.

————, "Automated Design Engineering," *Datamation,* June 1964.

"IBM Demonstrates System to Aid Computerized Design," *Steel,* November 9, 1964.

Johnson, Walter, "IBM Reports on Major Advance in EDP Memory Technology," *Electronic News,* October 25, 1965.

Kinowlton, Kenneth C., "Computer-Produced Movies," *Science,* November 26, 1965.

Langefors, Borje, "Automated Design," *International Science and Technology,* February 1964.

"Man-Computer Teams Add New Dimension to Design," *Steel,* May 10, 1965.

"Man vs. Machine," *Engineering News,* December 10, 1964.

Merris, Dora, "New Approaches to Computer-Aided Design," *Product Engineering,* February 3, 1964.

Moffett, Thurber J., Grant D. Christensen, Jay S. Crawford, and William W. Thomas, "Is Automation of the Engineering Department Here?" *Engineering Graphics,* November 1965.

Moffet, Thurber J., "Thinking Out Loud," feature in *Engineering Graphics,* January and February 1966.

Peterfreund, Stanley, "Automation Can Be Pleasant," *International Management,* February 1965.

"Piping by Computer," *Chemical Week,* May 23, 1964.

Prince, M. D., S. H. Chasen, *et al.,* "Computer-Aided Design," *Lockheed-Georgia Quarterly,* Summer 1965.

"Programming Advance Aims at Do-It-Yourself Computer Solving," *Engineering News,* October 10, 1963.

Veinott, C. G., "Electric Machinery Design by Digital Computer," *Electric Engineering,* April 1963.

Warshawsky, Edwin H., "Design by Computer," *Industrial Research,* October 1965.

PUBLISHED AND UNPUBLISHED PAPERS

Arnold, John E., "The Role of Design in Automation," Manufacturing Series No. 205, American Management Association, New York, 1953.

The Case for Good Design, Management Bulletin 35, American Management Association, New York, 1963.

Chasen, S. H., "The Introduction of Man-Computer Graphics into the Aerospace Industry," *Proceedings—Fall Joint Computer Conference, 1965,* Spartan Books, Inc., Baltimore, 1965.

"Computer-Aided Design for Numerical Control Systems" and "Computer-Aided Design of Electronic Circuits," *Annual Report, 1964-1965,* Electronic Systems Laboratory, Department of Electrical Engineering, Massachusetts Institute of Technology.

Coons, S. A., "An Outline of the Requirements for a Computer-Aided Design System," *Proceedings—Spring Joint Computer Conference, 1963,* Spartan Books, Inc., Baltimore, 1963.

Fetter, William A., "Computer Graphics in Engineering Communication," a presentation to the 1963 Engineering Institute on Design and Drafting Automation, University of Wisconsin.

Fitzgerald, Ed L., "Digigraphics—the background, the concept, and the potential impact of this new technology on engineering and science," Control Data Corporation, Digigraphics Laboratories, Burlington, Mass., January 1966.

Garrity, John T., "Getting the Most Out of Your Computer," McKinsey and Company, Inc.

Hamilton, MacKenzie L., and Abbot D. Weiss, "An Approach to Computer-Aided Preliminary Ship Design," Technical Memorandum ESL-TM-228, Electronic System Laboratory, Department of Electrical Engineering, Massachusetts Institute of Technology, January 1965.

Harris, Herbert R., and O. Dale Smith, "AUTODRAFT—A Language and Processor for Design and Drafting," a presentation to the *SHARE-Design Automation Workshop,* Atlantic City, New Jersey, June 24, 1965.

Hawarn, Wayne Carl, "CAD of Slender Structural Members," unpublished masters thesis at Massachusetts Institute of Technology, 1964.

Herzog, B., "Graphic Information Processing Input and Output to Computers," an informal summary based on two speeches, Systems Research Office, Ford Motor Company, September 1965.

Jacks, Edwin L., and associates, *The GM DAC-I System, Design Augmented by Computers,* five papers presented at the 1964 Fall Joint Computer Conference, Computer Technology Department, Research Laboratories, General Motors Corporation, October 28, 1964. Titles of the papers are: "A Laboratory for the Study of Graphical Man-Machine Communication," "Operational Software in a Disk-Oriented System," "Image Processing Hardware for a Man-Machine Graphical Communication," "Input/Output Software Capability for a Man-Machine Communication and Image Processing System," "A Line-Scanning System Controlled from an On-Line Console."

Johnson, T. E., "SKETCHPAD III—A Computer Program for Drawing in Three Dimensions," *Proceedings—Spring Joint Computer Conference, 1963,* Spartan Books, Inc., Baltimore, 1963.

Joyce, John D., "Input of Graphics," a paper from Computer Technology Department, General Motors Research Laboratories, Warren, Michigan, May 1965.

Mann, Robert W., "Engineering Specifications for a Man-Computer System for Design," a paper presented at the University of Michigan-University of

Detroit, Engineering Summer Conference, "Application of Computers to Automated Design," August 3-7, 1964.

Mann, R. W. and S. A. Coons, "Computer-Aided Design," *McGraw-Hill Yearbook of Science and Technology,* McGraw-Hill Book Company, New York, 1965.

Roos, Daniel, "ICES Systems Design—Objectives, Requirements, and Components," Technical Report T65-8, Department of Civil Engineering, School of Engineering, Massachusetts Institute of Technology, August 20, 1965.

Ross, D. T. and J. E. Rodriquez, "Theoretical Foundations for the Computer-Aided Design System," *Proceedings—Spring Joint Computer Conference, 1963,* Spartan Books, Inc., Baltimore, 1963.

Ross, D. T., S. A. Coons, and J. E. Ward, "Investigations in Computer-Aided Design for Numerically Controlled Production," Interim Engineering Report ESL-IR-241, Electronic Systems Laboratory, Electrical Engineering Department, Massachusetts Institute of Technology, June 1965.

Simon, Herbert A., "The Corporation: Will It Be Managed By Machines?" in Anshen, Melvin, and George L. Bach, eds., *Management and Corporations 1985,* McGraw-Hill Book Company, New York, 1960.

Stotz, Robert, "Man-Machine Console Facilities for Computer-Aided Design," *Proceedings—Spring Joint Computer Conference, 1963,* Spartan Books, Inc., Baltimore, 1963.

Stuckles, Tom O., III, "Some Human Engineering Problems in Computer-Aided Design," a thesis at Massachusetts Institute of Technology, 1964.

Sutherland, I. E., "SKETCHPAD—A Man-Machine Graphical Communication System," *Proceedings—Spring Joint Computer Conference, 1963,* Spartan Books, Inc., Baltimore, 1963.

Weiner, Jerome I., "The Impact of Technological Change on Design," Unpublished Notes, Massachusetts Institute of Technology, 1965.

MISCELLANEOUS

"The Engineer and the Computer" and other articles in *Computing Report for the Scientist and Engineer,* December 1965, Data Processing Division, International Business Machines Corporation, White Plains, N. Y.

"PL/1: Powerful Programming Aid," *Computing Report for the Scientist and Engineer,* August 1965, Data Processing Division, International Business Machines Corporation, White Plains, N. Y.